JAMES HILLMAN

pan
and the nightmare

SPRING PUBLICATIONS
THOMPSON, CONN.

Published by Spring Publications
Thompson, Conn.
www.springpublications.com

"First published in 1972

The translation of "Ephialtes" is published under license from B.G. Teubner Verlag, Wiesbaden, Germany, who reserves all rights on behalf of the Roscher heirs."

Third, revised edition 2020 (v. 1.2)

ISBN: 978-0-88214-088-9

Library of Congress Control Number: 2020916217

CONTENTS

PART TWO

Ephialtes –
A Pathological-Mythological Treatise on the Nightmare
in Classical Antiquity
WILHELM HEINRICH ROSCHER

ACKNOWLEDGMENTS

The translation of "Ephialtes" was made by A.V.O'Brien in Vienna in 1963–64 and edited there by A.K.O. Donoghue, who, although foreseeing the difficulties ahead, nevertheless also foresaw the value of the undertaking. He, together with Renate Welch, grappled with most of the references. The final version was prepared for publication by Murray Stein, with the assistance of James Fenwick for the transliterations of Greek words. Patricia Berry edited my essay; Valerie Donleavy designed and supervised the book's production. I am grateful to Rafael López-Pedraza for conversations on the Pan theme, and to James Redfield who, at the University of Chicago in 1968, read through the translation and an earlier sketch of the essay suggesting improvements for its revised form.

I wish to also acknowledge my debt to books (mentioned throughout this volume in appropriate places) by Ernest Jones, Reinhard Herbig, and Patricia Merivale in whose essential works for this theme the necessary scholarly references can be found, and, lastly, my debt to Wilhelm Heinrich Roscher.

J.H.
Zurich, 1971

The scholarly works by Philippe Borgeaud and Roberto Malini (referenced in the text) need to be mentioned.

J.H.
Thompson, 2000

PART ONE

An Essay on Pan

A NEW REVISED EDITION

James Hillman

Socrates: Beloved Pan, and all you other gods who haunt this place, give me beauty in the inward soul; and may the outward and inward man be at one.
—Plato, *Phaedrus,* 279*b*

For the true significance of the Nightmare to be properly appreciated, first by the learned professions and then by the general public, would in my opinion entail consequences, both scientific and social, to which the term momentous might well be applied. What is at issue is nothing less than the very meaning of religion itself.
—Ernest Jones, *On the Nightmare* (1931)

The Psyche's Return to Greece

[I]nner motives spring from a deep source that is not made by consciousness and is not under its control. In the mythology of earlier times these forces were called *mana,* or spirits, demons, and gods. They are as active today as they ever were. If they conform to our wishes we call them happy hunches or impulses... If they go against us then we say that it is just bad luck, or that certain people are against us, or that the cause of our misfortunes must be pathological. The one thing we refuse to admit is that we are dependent upon "powers" that are beyond our control.[1]

If tendencies toward dissociation were not inherent in the human psyche, fragmentary psychic systems would never have been split off; in other words, neither spirits nor gods would have ever come into existence. That is also the reason why our time has become so utterly godless and profane: we lack all knowledge of the unconscious psyche and pursue the cult of consciousness to the exclusion of all else.

Our true religion is a monotheism of consciousness, a possession by it, coupled with a fanatical denial of the existence of fragmentary autonomous systems.[2]

When the monotheism of consciousness is no longer able to deny the existence of fragmentary autonomous systems and no longer able to deal with our actual psychic state, then there arises the fantasy of returning to Greek polytheism. For the "return to Greece" offers a way of coping when our centers cannot hold and things fall apart. The polytheistic alternative does not set up conflicting opposites between beast and Bethlehem, between chaos and unity; it permits the coexistence of all the psychic fragments and gives them patterns in the imagination of Greek mythology. A "return to Greece" was experienced in ancient Rome itself, and in the Italian Renaissance, and in the Romantic psyche during the times of revolution. In recent years it has been an intrinsic part of the lives of such artists and thinkers as Stravinsky, Picasso, Heidegger, Joyce, and Freud. The "return to Greece" is a psychological response to the challenge of breakdown; it offers a model of disintegrated integration.

Enough has been written to justify the "return to Greece" from aesthetic, philosophical, and cultural points of view. Our culture has tended to look to Greece for past glory, for perfection, grace, and clarity of mind, and also when in search of "origins," for Greece is where our culture began. But our aim here is to look to Greece for psychological insight. We are trying to understand both what is this "Greece" that so draws the psyche and what the psyche finds there.

When the dominant vision that holds a period of culture together cracks, consciousness regresses into earlier containers, seeking sources for survival which also offer sources of revival. Critics are right when they see the "return to Greece" as a regressive death wish, as escape from contemporary conflicts into mythologies and speculations of a fantasy world. But looking backward makes it possible to move forward, for looking backward revives the fantasy of the child archetype, *fons et origo*, who is both the moment of helpless weakness and the future unfolding. "Renaissance" (rebirth) would be a senseless word without the implied dissolution, the very death out of which that rebirth comes. Critics miss the validity and necessity of regression. Critics also miss the necessity of a regression that is particularly "Greek."

Our culture shows two alternative paths for regression. These paths have been called Hellenism and Hebraism, and they represent the psychological alternatives of multiplicity and unity. We see the alternatives at critical junctures of Western history, for instance at the time of the decline of Rome, which accompanied Constantine into Christianity (as Hebraism had then been renamed). We see them again at the times of the Renaissance and Reformation, when south Europe returned to Hellenism and northern Europe returned to Hebraism.

Hebraism reconfirms the monotheism of ego-consciousness, This path suits when the consciousness of an era or of an individual senses that its survival is best served by an archetypal pattern of heroism and unity. The early image of Christ was compounded with the military Mithra and the muscular Hercules, and Constantine's conversion, which finally turned the tide against classical polytheism, was heralded by a martial vision which came to him before he set forth into battle. Similarly the Hebraism of the Reformation, despite its tolerance for protest, variety, and splittings, is archetypally inspired by the fantasy of unified heroic strength; the individual is conceived as an undivided unit of arm-bearing responsibility who stands before God, one to one, the primal encounter. Today, the monocentric path is followed whenever we try to resolve a crisis in the soul by means of ego psychology, whenever we try to "reform."

The psyche in crisis has, of course, other fantasies. Hellenism's many and Hebraism's one are not the only ways out of the psyche's pathological dilemma. There is flight into futurism and its technologies, turning East and inward, going primitive and natural, moving upward and out altogether in transcendence. But these alternatives are less authentic. They are simplistic; they neglect our history and the claims of its images upon us; and they urge escaping from the plight rather than deepening it by providing it with cultural background and differentiated structure.

Science fictions and the fictions of science, instruction from American Indians or Oriental counselors—brilliant and wise as they all may be—fail to remind us of our Western imaginal history, of the actual images at work in our souls. By circumventing our imaginal tradition, they cut us off even further from it. Then the alternative paths to Hebraism and Hellenism work as repressions, actually adding to the soullessness which their images would help to repair.

Hebraism fails to meet the present dilemma simply because it is too well established, too identical with our moralistic world view: there is a Bible in every wanderer's bedroom, where there might better be the *Odyssey*. We can find no renewal in our ego's conscious tradition, only reinforcement for drying habits of a monocentric mind that would hold its universe together with guilt-making, self-improving sermons.

Hellenism, however, brings the tradition of the unconscious imagination; Greek polytheistic complexity bespeaks our complicated and unknown psychic situations. Hellenism furthers revival by offering wider space and another sort of blessing to the full range of images, feelings, and peculiar moralities that are our actual psychic natures. They need no deliverance from evil if they are not imagined to be evil in the first place.

If in our disintegration we cannot put all our bits into one monotheistic ego psychology, or cannot delude ourselves with the progressive futurism or the natural primitivism that once worked so well, and if we need a complexity to match our sophistication, then we return to Greece. "No other mythology known to us—developed or primitive, ancient or modern—is marked by quite the same complexity and systematic quality as the Greek."[3] Greece provides a polycentric pattern of the most richly elaborated polytheism of all cultures,[4] and so is able to hold the chaos of the secondary personalities and autonomous impulses of a field, a time, or an individual. This fantastic variety offers the psyche manifold fantasies for reflecting its many possibilities.

Behind and within all Greek culture—in art, thought, and action—is its mythical polycentric background. This was the psychic imaginal world from which came the "glory that was Greece." This mythical background was perhaps less bound to ritual and actual religious cults than were the mythologies of other high cultures. In other words, Greek myth serves less specifically as a religion and more generally as a psychology, working in the soul as both the stimulus and the differentiated container for the extraordinary psychic richness of ancient Greece.

But the "Greece" to which we return is not literal; it includes all periods from Minoan to Hellenistic, all localities from Asia Minor to Sicily. This "Greece" refers to a historical and geographical psychic region, a fantasy or mythic Greece, an inner Greece of the mind that is only indirectly connected with actual geography and actual history—so that these then become devalued. "[U]ntil the age of Romanticism, Greece was no more than a museum inhabited by people beyond contempt."[5]

Petrarch, who in the fourteenth century did more than anyone to revive the literature of antiquity, could not read Greek. Winckelmann in the eighteenth century, who did more than anyone to revive classicism and who invented the modern worship of Greece, never set foot there and may never have seen an original major piece of Greek sculpture. Nor did Racine go there, nor Goethe, Hölderlin, Hegel, Heine, Keats, or even Nietzsche. Yet they all reconstituted "Greece" in their works. Byron is the absurd—and fatal—exception. Of course, Greek language, literature, politics, and science were known during those centuries, Socrates was worshipped, statuary, architecture, and metrics copied, but few went to the empirical Greece and rarely did anyone even go to the original Greek texts. It was the "emotion charged image of Greece" that held sway.[6] And this image has maintained its charge of emotion by means of a continuing body of myths (the "Greek myths" and the metaphor of "Greece"), persisting in consciousness from post-Hellenic times until today.

"Greece" persists as an inscape rather than a landscape, a metaphor for the imaginal realm in which the archetypes as gods have been placed. We may therefore read all the documents and fragments of myth left from antiquity also as accounts or witnesses of the imaginal. Archeology becomes archetypology, pointing less to a literal history than to eternal actualities of the imagination, speaking to us of what is going on now in psychic reality.

The return to Greece is neither to a historical time in the past nor to an imaginary time, a utopian Golden Age that was or may come again. Instead "Greece" offers us a chance to revision our souls and psychology by means of imaginal places and persons rather than time. We move out of temporal thinking and historicity altogether, to an imaginal region, a differentiated archipelago of locations, *where* the gods are and not *when* they were or will be.

Quarrels may arise between Greece as fact and as fantasy, since historical and literary scholarship traditionally views its Greece literally, each generation of scholars delighting in seeing through the fanciful interpretation of the facts perpetrated by the generation preceding. Indeed, it may be said that the inner Greece of the imagination affects the perspectives of classical scholarship—a field so engrossed in the buried, the broken, the remnant, in unknown roots and origins, in myths and gods, that it is especially subject to the influence of the archetypes in the arrangement and interpretation of its "facts." The gods seem to do battle in this very field and, owing to that archetypal passion, the dead languages, which have a hard time to prove rationally their relevance for today, are kept vital by the psyche itself because of their importance for the imagination.

We return to Greece in order to rediscover the archetypes of our mind and of our culture. Fantasy returns there to become archetypal. By stepping back into the mythic, the nonfactual, and nonhistorical, the psyche can reimagine its factual, historical predicaments from another vantage point. Greece becomes the multiple magnifying mirror in which the psyche recognizes its persons and processes in configurations that are larger than life but bear on the life of our secondary personalities.[7]

Imagination is key.

When we speak, Greek is inside our words; when we think, construct, calculate, and organize, Greece is forming our minds. Even the idea of an idea is Greek. This truth does not deny the values inherited from other cultures, their great gods, their images, their souls. However to relativize "Greece" as just one cultural influence, to punish it for being too Western, white, male, hierarchical, and far in the past is to fall into racist literalism. By this I mean a series of errors. First, it is an error to identify imagination with geography, psychology with sociology, and time with causality (e.g., since Chinese, African, Egyptian, and Semitic cultures are older they must be preeminent in our psyches). Second, it is an error to confine the psyche to genetic inheritance; for your mind is determined neither by your blood nor your skin. And third, and perhaps most grave, it is an error to personalize the psyche into what your personal opinions consider relevant for your personal problems, which is a common way to avoid digging into the archetypal roots of imagination in collective history, roots that affect your problems well below your awareness. Whether we are Tibetan or Jamaican, from the Red Sea or Yellow, without a trace of actual Greece in our bones or an inkling of Greek myths, because we are inescapably and undeniably immersed in the overwhelming course of what has become Euro-American Atlantic civilization—its notions of laws and education, of technology and reasoning, of psyche and person—to know ourselves, we must return to Greece where that very idea itself finds first location.

There is good reason Pan shall be the guide for this return to the imagination of Greece—that kind of mind preceding Christianized civilization. Plutarch's (ca. 46–120 CE) famous report that the Great God Pan died coincides with the ascension of Christianity. Legends, images, and theology attest to an irreconcilable conflict between Pan and Christ, a tension that has never ended in that the Devil with his horns and hooves and hair is none other than old Pan as seen in the Christian mirror.

The death of one is the life of the other. This contrast appears again in the symbolization of their bodies, their geographies, their rhetorics. The one has the cave, the other the Mount; the one music, the other Word; Pan's legs leap and dance, yet they are crooked, hairy, and goat-footed; Jesus's legs are broken and stretched, his feet crossed and nailed. Jesus, the Good Shepherd; Pan, the obstreperous, unruly goat. Pan is naked and phallic; Jesus, circumcised, covered, and asexual.

The Pan/Jesus conflict presents immense difficulties for the individual in our civilization. How might one overcome the historical hindrances so as to reenter the pagan imagination of Pan and his nature without falling into a wild Satanist cult? We cannot simply dump our history, but must wrestle with its prejudices.

In his famous essay "Culture and Anarchy," Matthew Arnold defines this prejudice: "The governing idea of Hellenism," he writes, "is *spontaneity of consciousness*; that of Hebraism, *strictness of conscience*."[8] Therefore the spontaneous phenomena of Pan—panic, sexual urges, nightmares—are encountered moralistically. We are told to fight the good fight against bad impulses.

Western history has left us with two equally repugnant alternatives. Either we worship an Arcadian Pan of sentimentalized Nature who offers liberation from that history, or we curse him as a pagan demon who threatens civilization with anarchic atavism and other excesses with psychological labels such as shadow, acting out, exhibitionism, or id. The way each of us responds to the calls of Pan and is guided by him into the territory of "Greece" depends largely upon the Christian twist within our deeply cherished attitudes.

Thus it seems that the sole possibility for crossing the bridge into an imagination of antiquity requires us to set aside those prejudiced perspectives that we have ennobled as "civilized" and which go on repeating the death of Pan by both sentimentalizing and demonizing him at one and the same time.

Rafael López-Pedraza has shown in his "Tale of Dryops and the Birth of Pan"[9] that the revival of Pan and the realm we call the imaginal, mythical, and Greek begins with the manifestations of Pan in the private sphere of one's own reactions to his phenomena: rape, masturbation, nightmare panic, seduction by nymphs, and other Pan-induced events that force us out of civilized habits. These are the modes by which Pan's music reaches us today. These are the ways of the return, the epistrophe into imagination. Thus the return to Greece is neither a nostalgic idealization, an aesthetic romanticism, nor a distancing structuralist study of symbolism. Rather it is a descent into the cave.

1. *C.G. Jung, Man and his Symbols* (1961), 82. [Cf. *Collected Works of C.G. Jung* (= *CW,* cited by paragraph numbers), trans. R.F.C. Hull, 20 vols. (Princeton, N.J.: Princeton University Press, 1953–79), 18: 554]. To set the stage for this inquiry into one of our history's most strange divine figures, Pan, and one of our psyche's most terrifying experiences, the nightmare, we will begin with two passages from Jung and a long one of mine.

2. *CW* 13: 51 (italics mine).

3. G.S. Kirk, *Myth: It's Meaning and Function in Ancient and Other Cultures* (Berkeley and Los Angeles: University of California Press, 1970), 205.

4. G. van der Leeuw, *Religion in Essence and Manifestation,* 2 vols. (New York: Harper & Row, 1963).

5. R. Weiss, *Renaissance Discovery of Classical Antiquity* (Oxford: Blackwell, 1969), 140.

6. J.M. Osborn, "Travel Literature and the Rise of Neo-Hellenism in England," *Bulletin of the New York Public Library* 67 (1963): 300.

7. The entirety of this passage is from my *Re-Visioning Psychology* (New York: Harper & Row, 1975), 27–30.

8. M. Arnold, *Culture and Anarchy: An Essay in Political and Social Criticism* (London: Smith, Elder and Co., 1869), 147.

9. *Spring: An Annual of Archetypal Psychology and Jungian Thought* (1976): 176–90.

The Dream in 1900

Having placed Pan within the context of the return to Greece, now we must place the nightmare within the context of dream theory, particularly as it was developing a hundred years ago when Roscher's monograph appeared. His monograph belongs among the works on dreams, which Freud reviews so carefully in the first section of his revolutionary *Traumdeutung*. It could not of course have been mentioned there since that work and this monograph were published but a few months apart. At the turn of the century, the dream was a subject of interest to many besides Freud. The nineteenth century witnessed a spate of writings upon the dream especially in France, Germany, and even in the United States. The literature of this period generally falls into three kinds, indicating the three distinct approaches to the dream that were then current.

The first approach was materialistic; it held that the dream was an echo in the mind of physiological events in the body. Dream images were the psychological translation of physical events. Research investigated the physical origins of dreams in sensations of coldness, wetness, etc., in subliminal and forgotten perceptions, in nitrous oxide; so too, there were investigations upon the physiological states during dreaming in order to discover the basis of the dream in somatic events. This view is still with us today when we attribute a dream to something we ate, to a late television stimulus, or to heavy blankets. It is also still with us on more sophisticated levels, as for instance when we assume that the physiological correlates of dream states (electrical patterns of brain activity, neuro-hormonal or circulatory changes) are the necessary and sufficient conditions of dreams.

The second view was rationalistic. It held that the dream made no sense at all, being a sort of derangement of the mental functions when they relaxed during sleep, like bits of mosaic falling apart without the cohesive cement of conscious willing and association. Thus dreams were akin to madness, a meaningless jumble of fragments that did not tell more about the person who dreamt them, but less. They were therefore not a proper subject for serious attention, let alone scientific investigation. The third, the Romantic view, can be found mainly in the works of poets, writers, and thinkers with a mystical bent—Novalis, Gérard de Nerval, Coleridge, Schubert, as has been discussed by Albert Béguin.[10] The Romantic view reflects in poetic and philosophical language the older religious view of archaic and traditional peoples that during sleep the mind or soul is open to occult powers. The dream was an avenue of communication with the gods; in sleep the psyche wandered, received intuitions and messages, could meet the dead in the beyond. Therefore, dreams were a source of inspiration and knowledge. They held real personal significance.

One of Freud's great accomplishments was to blend together these three contemporary illuminations of dream life into one brilliant theory. In agreement with the rationalists, he held that the dream did not make sense, *prima facie*. It was indeed nonsense on the manifest level, showing signs of dissociation, distortion, and condensation such as one finds in the products of the insane mind. However, like the Romantics, he thought that the dream could be deciphered; it contained a personal message with a meaning for the dreamer and was a *via regia* to "another world," the unconscious. He also accepted in part the position of the materialists, for he found the ultimate purpose of the dream to be in the psychophysiology of sleep (protecting sleep) and its ultimate source in somatic stimuli (sexual tensions). Freud's theory, by its very encompassing elegance, opened new perspectives while it eclipsed others, mainly the experimental and physiological. During the first fifty years after Freud, nearly all the literature on the dream was published by psychoanalysts. The new romantics were the professional dream interpreters, while the kind of dream research that had taken place in psychological laboratories previous to Freud faded to a tiny percentile of the literature on dreams. Dream interpretation was in the ascendancy over dream research. Today, the alternative approaches, which Freud united, are appearing again, and, as Freudian theory seems on the decline, no longer holding the mystical and the material together in a rational coherence, the trend seems to be moving out of the consulting room and back to the laboratory as the place for dream investigation. Perhaps we are again expecting a new synthesis, such as made by Freud in 1900, which can bind together the current interpretations of the dream as a manifestation of an archetypal substratum of the personality.

Roscher's study does suggest a movement in this direction, for he brings together fantasy and physical experience, dream and body reactions, behind both of which stands the figure of Pan. The archetype expresses itself as a pattern of behavior (panic and nightmare) and as a pattern of imagery (Ephialtes, Pan and his entourage). In other words, Roscher's work also suggests a method for psychosomatic investigation based on archetypal psychology. Such investigations would give, as does Roscher, primary place to patterns of fantasy as precisely described by mythology.

Therefore his little monograph, ostensibly a mythological study only, is a parallel work to Freud's *Traumdeutung* in that it offers a path for approaching the dream other than the psychological dreamwork elaborated by Freud. Roscher goes deeper even if he is less overtly psychological because his approach to dream events through Pan goes beyond personal psychodynamics. Pan cannot be remitted to any complex of one's personal life; he is not accountable through psychological explanation. Roscher's difference with Laistner and what ultimately became the Freudian tradition of dream theory may make this point clearer.

Roscher's approach to the nightmare takes off from the work of Ludwig Laistner. Roscher criticizes him and develops his ideas in contrast to Laistner. Ernest Jones, however, according to the index of his book *On the Nightmare*,[11] refers to Laistner thirty-one times (to Freud thirty-five times, to Roscher thrice). Although parts of Jones's work were written in 1910 and 1912, he did have ample time to use Roscher's study on the same theme, so that Jones's reliance upon Laistner, and Roscher's divergence from Laistner, point to two different views of the dream operative today.

Laistner (1845–1896) trained first for theology, but then moved into the field of Germanic studies and edited eight editions of Goethe's works in Stuttgart. He was particularly interested in German myths and grammar, and he examined folklore, fairytales, Greek and other European mythical figures, including "Mittagsfrauen" and other noon demons. His ideas on the nightmare appear in his untranslated two-volume *Das Rätsel der Sphinx* (The Riddle of the Sphinx), published in Berlin, 1889. This is mainly an investigation of dreams on the one hand and folklore and fairytale on the other. Jones says of this work:

In it he took the clinical characteristics of the Nightmare and with extraordinary ingenuity traced them through a very large series of myths. There was of course at that time (1889) no knowledge of the unconscious layers of the mind, so that today the chief value of his work is a casuistic one. Partly because of certain philological difficulties, Laistner's work was unduly neglected by mythologists, though before Freud's attempt it should be counted as perhaps the most serious attempt to place mythology on a naturalistically intelligible basis.[12]

It would seem that the difference between Roscher and Laistner is one which still exists in psychology, and not only in regard to the interpretation of the nightmare. Roscher blames Laistner for his attempt, which did not succeed, to raise the dream "and in particular the nightmare, to the main and fundamental principle of all mythology." For Laistner, as for Freud and Jones after him, there is a psychological, naturalistic ground for myth and religion. Laistner points to the erotic character of these dreams, comparable with Freud and Jones who later can reduce mythology and religion to psychological mechanisms connected with sexuality. Roscher, on the other hand, is primarily a mythologist who would not reduce the mythic to intrapersonal processes.

Even when he uses the rationalistic fallacies of his time, Roscher would more likely adhere to an attitude towards both dream and myth represented, albeit in different ways in a different age, by Jung, Kerényi, and Eliade. Myth and religion are not reducible to dreams, but both have their source in something transpersonal, in a reality that is not personally human, even if human in an archetypal sense. Myth and religion are sui generis aspects of life, and so also of nature. Just as sexuality is a sui generis function of the psyche (and not the psyche a derivative of sexuality), so too are the dreaming, the mythmaking, and the religious functions. They tell of each other, but they are not each other. Their tellings are myths and their connections with each other are by means of analogies, not because of a common root. Their base is not naturalistic, as Jones says, for nature is itself a metaphor; therefore, to understand the dream we must speak as it speaks, not in natural concepts but in images. Consequently, our fundamental metaphor in my essay, as well as in Roscher's, whether it be for the dream or for Pan, is not "natural" but "imaginal."

10. A. Béguin, *L'Âme romantique et le rêve: essai sur le romantisme allemand et la poésie française* (Paris: J. Corti, 2006).

11. E. Jones, *On the Nightmare* (London: Hogarth Press, 1931).

12. Ibid., 73.

Pan, Goat-God of Nature

Roscher's thesis, briefly is that the nightmare demon in antiquity is te great god Pan in any of his several forms, and that the experience of the nightmare demon then was similar to that reported in the psychiatry and psychology of Roscher's own day. Having established this, Roscher leaves it. But we might go further, concluding that Pan is still alive. We experience him mainly through psychopathological disturbances, other modes having been lost in our culture.

Thus we may expect him in the psychotherapist's consulting room, and indeed there is evidence of his appearance there.[13] This conclusion accords with a thesis elaborated in many of my works: the repressed gods return as the archetypal core of symptom complexes. The relations between *mythos* and *pathos* are part of the larger task of exploring psychopathology in terms of archetypal psychology. One implication of this psychology is that mythology becomes an indispensable discipline for the training of psychotherapists. Roscher's monograph which links mythology and pathology in its very title would be a basic text for psychotherapy.

Because of the satyr-goat-phallus nature of Pan, both the panic anxiety of the nightmare and its erotic aspects can be subsumed by one and the same figure. In Roscher's treatment of the figure, Pan is not a projected image, a kind of psychopathological complex created by fantasy to express sexual anxiety. His is a mythical reality. Although Roscher falls prey at moments to the rationalist-materialist view of the dream presented by Borner (that goat-haired bedclothes and dyspnea give rise to the Pan experience), this "explanation" of the nightmare nevertheless still rests upon the epiphany of Pan, who always remains as a vivid reality in the pages of Roscher. What emerges from his essay is the genius insight: the entanglement, the very unity of the mythological and the pathological.

When Roscher discusses panic and nightmare in animals, he shows his awareness of the instinctual level of the nightmare—particularly its sexuality. We see in his writing the same struggle with the "sexual problem" that was emerging at that time through many of his psychological contemporaries, Havelock Ellis, Auguste Forel, Ivan Bloch, and of course Freud, to say nothing of the work of the painters and writers at the end of the century who were rediscovering the phallic goat-satyr in the deeper layers of human drive, and who, as did Freud with Oedipus and Roscher with Pan, expressed their insights in the configurations of Greek myth. Patricia Merivale, in her fine book,[14] has collected a staggering assortment of examples of the nineteenth century's devotion to Pan, the period in literature that she says saw his heyday. Pan, by the way, has been the favorite Greek figure in English poetry; he outdistances his nearest rivals (Helen, Orpheus, and Persephone) in statistical appearance nearly two to one.

Greek myth placed Pan as god of nature. What is meant by that word "nature" has been analyzed into at least fifty differing notions, so that our usage of "nature" here must be discerned from the qualities associated with Pan, with his description, his appearance in imagery, his style of behavior. All gods had aspects of nature and could be found in nature, leading some to conclude that antique mythological religion was essentially a nature religion, the transcendence of which by Christianity, therefore, meant the suppression especially of the representative of nature, Pan, who soon became the goat-footed Devil. To specify Pan's nature we shall have to see how Pan personifies it, both in his figure and in his landscape, which is at once an inscape, a metaphor and not mere geography. His original place, Arcadia, is both a physical and a psychic location. The "caves obscure" where he could be encountered ("The Orphic Hymn to Pan") were expanded upon by the Neoplatonists[15] as the material recesses where impulse resides, the dark holes of the psyche whence desire and panic arise.

His habitat in antiquity, like that of his later Roman shapes (Faunus, Silvanus) and companions, was always dells, grottos, water, woods, and wilds—ever villages, never the tilled and walled settlements of the civilized; cavern sanctuaries, not constructed temples. He was a shepherd's god, a god of fishers and hunters, a wanderer without even the stability provided by genealogy. The lexicographers of myth give at least twenty parentages of Pan.[16] He was possibly fathered by Zeus, Uranos, Kronos, Apollo, Odysseus, Hermes, or by Penelope's crowd of suitors. Hence his is a spirit that can arise from most anywhere, the product of many archetypal movements or by spontaneous generation. One tradition has him fathered by Aether, the tenuous substance that is invisible yet everywhere, and which word first meant bright sky or weather associated with Pan's hour of noon (see below). If so unspecific and spontaneous, then why attribute to him parentage at all. This line was taken by Apollodorus (Frag. 44b) and Servius (*On Virgil's "Georgia"*).

Certainly his maternal line is obscure. The main account from "The Homeric Hymn to Pan," and the one given by Kerényi in his *Gods of the Greeks,* has Pan abandoned at birth by his wood-nymph mother, but wrapped in a hare's pelt by his father Hermes (to be sired by Hermes emphasizes the mercurial element in Pan's background). Hermes took the babe to Olympus where he was accepted by all (*pan*) the gods with delight. Especially Dionysus enjoyed him.

This one tale places Pan within a specific configuration. First, enwrapped in the skin of the hare, an animal particularly sacred to Aphrodite, Eros, the Bacchic world, and the moon, implies his investment with those associations.[17] His initial garment means his initiation into their universe; he has been adopted by those structures of consciousness. Second, Hermes is his patron, giving Hermetic aspects to Pan's actions. They can be examined for messages. They are modes of communication, connections that mean something. Third, Dionysus's delight expresses the sympathy between them. These gods provide the archetypal cluster into which Pan fits and where we may most expect him to be constellated.

The mythologems—"the abandoned child," "wrapped in animal skin," and "pleasing to the gods"—may be pondered a long while. Their exegesis, which comes through living their meanings in our lives, may tell us much about our Pan-like behavior during moments of weakness and lostness (abandonment), as well as about our erotic *luxuria,* for, within the little love gage that the hare was, lies concealed in the uncultivated wilderness of Pan. What starts soft turns rough, and beneath the rabbit's fur lurks the goat. Yet the gods smile on our goatfooted child; they take it as a gift to the divine; they each find an affinity with it. Pan reflects them all.

As god of all nature, Pan personifies to our consciousness that which is all or only natural, behavior at its most nature-bound. Behavior that is nature-bound is, in a sense, divine. It is behavior transcendent to the human yoke of purposes, wholly impersonal, objective, ruthless. The cause of such behavior is obscure; it springs suddenly, spontaneously. As Pan's genealogy is obscure, so is the origin of instinct. To define instinct as an inborn release mechanism, or to speak of it as a chthonic spirit, a prompting of nature, puts into obscure psychological concepts the obscure experiences that might once have been attributed to Pan.

Above all we must remember that the Pan experience is beyond the control of the willing subject and his ego psychology. Even where the will is most disciplined and the ego most purposeful, and I am thinking now of men in battle, Pan appears, determining through panic the outcome of the fray. Twice in antiquity (at Marathon and against the Celts in 277 BCE) Pan appeared and the Greeks had their victory. He was commemorated with Nike. The panic flight is a protective reaction even if in its blindness the outcome can be mass death. The protective aspect of nature that appears in Pan shows not only in his affinity for herdsmen, nor in the word root (*pan*) of "pastor," "pastoral," and *pabulum* ("nourishment"), but as well in his role in the Dionysus train where Pan carries the shield of Dionysus on the march to India.[18]

In the Eros and Psyche tale told by Apuleius, Pan protects Psyche from suicide. The soul disconsolate, its love gone, divine help denied, panics. Psyche throws herself away, into the river that refuses her. In that same moment of panic, Pan appears with his reflective other side, Echo, and brings home to the soul some natural truths. Pan is both destroyer and preserver, and the two aspects appear to the psyche in close approximation. When we panic we can never know whether it may not be the first movement of nature that will yield—if we can hear the echo of reflection—a new insight into nature.

As Reinhard Herbig says in his monograph,[19] this god is always a goat, the goat always a divine force. Pan is not "represented" by a goat, nor is the goat "holy" to Pan; rather, Pan is the goat-god, and this configuration of animal-nature distinguishes nature by personifying it as something hairy, phallic, roaming and goatish. This Pan nature is no longer an idyllic display for the eye, something to walk through or long back to for sweetness. Nature as Pan is hot and close, his hairy animal smell, his erection, as if nature's arbitrary wayward force and uncanny mystery were summed into this one figure.

The "union of god and goat"—the phrase is from Nietzsche's *The Birth of Tragedy*—signified for the post-Nietzschean world the Dionysian mode of consciousness and the final diseased insanity of its promulgator. But though Nietzsche was speaking overtly of the goat-god, "in Nietzsche's biography," writes Jung,[20] "you will find irrefutable proof that the god he originally meant was really Wotan.[21] Thus, in attempting to understand the union of god and goat, which, as Merivale states,[22] is "the stable focal point of my investigations,"we must avoid confusing it with the Dionysus of Nietzsche in whose background was the Germanic Wotan.

Yet Nietzsche does penetrate one riddle of goat existence (and there are many, since the goat of the senex and the scapegoat and the Dionysian kid and the milk goat do not belong here) when he speaks of the horror of nature and the horror of individual existence. For the solitary goat is both the Oneness and the aloneness, a cursed nomadic existence in empty places, his appetite making them yet emptier, his song, "tragedy." This is not the fat, jolly Pan of some statuary or the elfin piper we call Peter or the "deep emotional self "of D. H. Lawrence's Pan, but the Pan of the Homeric hymn who in Chapman's Renaissance translation is called "leane and lovelesse."

The lechery, then, is secondary, and the fertility too; they arise from the dry longing of nature alone, of one who is ever an abandoned child and who in innumerable pairings is never paired, never fully changes the cleft hoof for rabbit's paw. He is called "unlucky in love," and we humans feel his sadness in nature's melancholy. There is a mournful tone of pipes in nature to which we retreat in romantic moments, yearning, lonely, and desperate. Pan may please the gods, but he never makes it to Olympus; he couples, but never wives; he makes music, but the muses favor Apollo.

13. For two examples of Pan in Jungian analysis, see R. Michel, "Die Gestalt des Pan und Träume der Gegenwart," Diss., C.G. Jung-Institut, Zurich, n.d.; and R. Blomeyer, "Die Konstellierung der Gegenüberstellung beim Auftauchen archetypischer Träume," *Zeitschrift für analytische Psychologie und ihre Grenzgebiete* 3.1 (1971).

14. P. Merivale, *Pan the Goat-God: His Myth in Modern Times* (Cambridge: Harvard University Press, 1969). Cf. R. Malini, *Pan dio della selva* (Milan: Edizioni dell'Ambrosino, 1998), for a remarkable anthology of classical passages and images.

15. See *Thomas Taylor the Platonist: Selected Writings,* ed. K. Raine and G.M. Harper (Princeton, N.J.: Princeton University Press, 1969), 225, 297ff.

16. Roscher wrote a separate study on this subject: "Die Sagen von der Geburt des Pan," *Philologus* 53 (1894): 362-77.

17. See John Layard, *The Lady of the Hare: Being a Study in the Healing Power of Dreams* (London: Faber and Faber, 1944), 212-20.

18. See Roscher, "Pan," in *Ausführliches Lexikon der griechischen und römischen Mythologie,* ed. W.H. Roscher, 6 vols, 4 supps. (Leipzig: B.G. Teubner, 1884-1937), vol. 3.1: 1388-90, for classical references to Pan the Warrior.

19. R. Herbig, *Pan—der griechische Bocksgott: Versuch einer Monographie* (Frankfurt am Main: Klostermann, 1949).

21. *CW* 11: 28.

21. See my "Dionysus in Jung's Writings," in *Mythic Figures,* Uniform Edition of the Writings of James Hillman, vol. 6 (Putnam, Conn.: Spring Publications, 2007), 15-30.

22. Merivale, *Pan the Goat-God,* 226.

Imaginal Reality

To grasp Pan as nature we must first be grasped by nature, both "out there" in an empty countryside, which speaks in sounds, not words, and "in here" in a startled reaction. (This pan no one has better recreated than D.H. Lawrence.) Uncanny as the goat's eye, nature comes at us in the instinctual experiences that Pan personifies. But to speak of "personification" does the god injustice, since it implies that man makes the gods and that nature is an impersonal abstract field of forces, such as thought conceives it.

Whereas, the demonic shape of Pan turns the concept "nature" into an immediate psychic shock. Western philosophical tradition from its beginnings in the Pre-Socratics and in the Old Testament has been prejudiced against images (*phantasia*) in favor of thought-abstractions. In the period since Descartes and the Enlightenment conceptualization has held preeminence; the psyche's tendency to personify has been disdainfully put down as anthropomorphism. One of the main arguments against the mythical mode of thinking has been that it works in images that are subjective, personal, sensuous. This above all must be avoided in Western epistemology, and so in descriptions of the forces of nature. To personify has meant to think animistic ally, primitively, pre-logically. The senses deceive; images that would relay truth about the world must be purified of their anthropomorphic elements. The only persons in the universe are human persons. Yet the experience of the gods, of heroes, nymphs, demons, angels and powers, of sacred animals, places, and things, as persons indeed precedes the concept of personification. It is not that we personify, but that the epiphanies come as persons.

Could we step back from our times, step out of the pretensions of the fearing ego who would bring every atom of nature under its control? Then we might realize again that we are not the source of personified gods. We do not make them up, anymore than we invent the sounds we hear in the woods, the hoof prints in the sand, the nightmare pressure weighing on our chests.

For millennia and most everywhere, it was palpably evident that divine and daimonic figures appeared as persons. But the scientific *Weltanschauung* with its cut between observer and observed severed us from that witness, and its testimony became magical thinking, primitive belief, superstition, insanity. Since the imaginal figures still occasionally broke in among the brightest and best educated, as in nightmares, these figures had to be made up by us. They could not be allowed their autonomy, else the scientific universe itself could become a nightmare.

Classical scholarship, seduced by the reductive method of science, quickly joined in to explain these apparitions as "projections" and "illusions" made up "unconsciously" by the perceiver. So, we find still, in Phillipe Borgeaud's excellent monograph,[23] an explanation of Pheidippides's direct encounter with Pan (on this messenger's run back to Athens from Marathon) as "only a projection of his wish." "It is not hard to imagine his tension, depression, and exhaustion by the time when, on his third day of constant running, he encountered the god Pan."

As the nightmare must derive from indigestion or a too-heavy quilt, so Pan must derive from physical dysfunction during a marathon run! Here scholarship not only fails its subject, it even denies the authority of the text[24] that it is explaining. Herodotus says Pan burst in on Pheidippides, cried out his name, and gave him a crucial message that saved Athens. The leaders of Athens believed Pheidippides, won the battle, and set up the Cult of Pan in Athens. Were the cunning and intelligent Greeks so deluded? Did all this come about because of the exhausted state of mind of a certain messenger who had a sudden bright idea and conjured up "Pan" to bless it with authority?

In his brilliant, thorough, and devastating critique of reductive falsification of "what actually happened," Charles Boer writes:

> [T]his was one of the greatest moments in the history of Western civilization, this apparition of a goat-footed God on the eve of a world-transforming battle, his message of help actually making a momentous difference in the course of events that led to the saving of democracy itself. It is just that no one today—especially professional mythologists—is permitted by the increasing constraints of the subject to take the story seriously anymore. Is the origin of democracy so small a matter, or is something wrong with mythologists?

You can take Pan's presence on the eve of Marathon "psychologically" (many ways), you can take it "symbolically," you can even take it "historically" in a twisted way (in which you account for the fact of the result, but dismiss the cause as mistaken). But you cannot take it seriously. Something else (if anything at all) must have happened, the scholars say, then what Pheidippides said happened.

...People on the other side of fifth-century Greece were of course privileged—and privileging!—to take Pan as the splendid imaginal reality he was. Imaginal figures were "visible" to them, heard by them, touched by them. They were not, at least in their eyes, "making this up."[25]

Precisely this we learn from Roscher, in spite of himself. For Roscher, like his contemporaries (e.g., Ameling on personification), tended to conceive Pan as a composite embodiment of the rough and fearful qualities of nature, just as his charming nymphs were visions of nature's tender, graceful, and lyrical seductiveness. But Roscher's conceptual framework taken from empirical associationist psychology (ideas are bundles of sense perceptions) does not accord with what he discovered in the empirical reports about nightmare demons. They are not a reassembly of frightening qualities, personifications *post hoc* of bed-clothes sensations. They are vividly real persons.

Dilthey insisted that personification was essential for humanistic understanding in contradistinction to scientific explanation, whose method requires conceptualization and definition. Lou Andreas-Salomé, following Dilthey, urged Freud to maintain this method of procedure essential to advance psychoanalysis as a humanistic rather than scientific psychology. Jung built his psychology upon the archetypes, which, though describable conceptually, are experienced and even named as persons. Jung went against the current of the times, moreover, by standing for images as primary data of the psyche and then taking these images at their sensuous emotional level, as the empirical phenomena that they are, and not as personifications of abstract ideas.

Dream language (as the nightmare shows), delusional and hallucinatory language, and folk language speak in terms of persons. So must a psychology that would talk to the psyche in its own speech. Jung's movement away from abstract concept and toward sensible person corresponds with the movement from intellect to imagination which is peopled with palpable sense images. Roscher's monograph—by stressing the person of Pan—contributes to that rediscovery of the imaginal which came to be known as the psychology of the unconscious, one of whose essential methodological departures from philosophy and science has been its language of personification.

A cry went through late antiquity: "Great Pan is dead!" Plutarch reported it in his "On the Failure of the Oracles."[26] The saying has itself become oracular, meaning many things to many people in many ages. One thing was announced: nature had become deprived of its creative voice. It was no longer an independent living force of generativity. What had had soul, lost it; lost was the psychic connection with nature. With Pan dead, so, too, was Echo; we could no longer capture consciousness through reflecting within our instincts. They had lost their light and fell easily to asceticism, following sheepishly without instinctual rebellion their new shepherd, Christ, with his new style of managed care. Nature no longer spoke to us—or we could no longer hear. The person of Pan the mediator, like an ether that invisibly enveloped all natural things with personal meaning, with brightness, had vanished. Stones became only stones—trees, trees; things, places, and animals no longer were this god or that, but became "symbols" or were said to "belong" to one god or another. When Pan is alive then nature is too, and it is filled with gods, so that the owl's hoot is Athene and the mollusk on the shore is Aphrodite. These bits of nature are not merely attributes or belongings. They are the gods in their biological forms. And where better to find the gods than in the things, places, and animals that they inhabit, and how better to participate in them than through their concrete natural presentations. Whatever was eaten, smelled, walked upon, or watched, all were sensuous presences of archetypal significance.

When Pan is dead, then nature can be controlled by the will of the new god, man, modeled in the image of Prometheus or Hercules, creating from it and polluting in it without a troubled conscience. (Hercules, who cleaned up Pan's natural world first, clubbing instinct with his will-power, does not stop to clear away the dismembered carcasses left to putrefy after his civilizing, creative tasks. He strides on to the next task, and ultimate madness.) As the human loses personal connection with personified nature and personified instinct, the image of Pan and the image of the Devil merge. Pan never died, say many commentators on Plutarch, he was repressed. Therefore as suggested above, Pan still lives, and not merely in the literary imagination. He lives in the repressed which returns, in the psychopathologies of instinct which assert themselves, as Roscher indicates, primarily in the nightmare and its associated erotic, demonic, and panic qualities.

Thus the nightmare indeed gives the clue to the re-approximation to lost, dead nature. In the nightmare, repressed nature returns, so close, so real that we cannot but react to it naturally, that is, we become wholly physical, possessed by Pan, screaming out, asking for light, comfort, contact. The immediate reaction is demonic emotion. We are returned by instinct to instinct.

23. P. Borgeaud, *The Cult of Pan in Ancient Greece,* trans. K. Atlass and J. Redfield (Chicago: The University of Chicago Press, 1988), 133.

24. Herodotus, 6.105.

25. C. Boer, "Watch Your Step," *Spring: A Journal of Archetype and Culture* 59 (1996): 104.

26. Plutarch, *De defectu oraculorum,* 17.

"Instinct"

Like many psychological words we use daily—soul, human, emotion, spirit, consciousness, feeling—instinct is more a metaphor, even if in conceptual dress, than a concept. Perhaps it is an idea in the original sense of that term where it meant "to see," so that by means of this word "instinct" we are able to see certain kinds of behavior, both looking upon it as an observer and looking into it, insighting it, as a participant. There is much spilled ink, and milk, about instinct, some regarding it as a primordial intelligence knowing more about life than we can ever learn, others taking it as the opposite of intelligence, something mechanical, archaic, and without any possibility for transformation. To it has been ascribed the best and the worst in human nature—and this gives us the hint for how we shall approach it here. For if Pan is the god of nature "in here," then he is our instinct. Again, since all gods partake of nature and have their mimesis in human nature, in our modes of fantasy, thought and behavior, of course Pan is not all instinct any more than he is all the gods. Which aspects of instinct he is, or which aspects of nature he is like, can only be discerned from the study of his phenomenology.

One major line of thought holds that instinctual behavior is characterized mainly by compulsion, often called the "all-or-none reaction." Beyond the primary biological processes—tropisms, ingestion and elimination, reproduction, cell growth, division and death, etc.—animal life as behavior moves automatically between the two poles of approach and retreat. A basic polarity of organic rhythm has been presented again and again through the centuries. One and the same archetypal idea about the rhythm of natural life occurs in those pairs called at different times and by different theorists: *accessum/recessum,* attraction/repulsion, *Lust/Unlust,* diastole/systole, introversion/extroversion, compulsion/inhibition, fusion/separation, all-or-none, etc. Under the domination of "inborn release mechanisms" (as instinct is also often called), patterns of approach and retreat become compulsive, undifferentiated, unreflective.

The two opposing positions regarding instinct—that it is intelligent and that it is not—have been combined in Jung's theory. He describes two ends to instinctual behavior: at the one, a compulsive archaic behavior pattern; at the other, archetypal images. Thus, instinct acts and at the same time forms an image of its action. The images trigger the actions; the actions are patterned by the images. Consequently, any transformation of the images affects the patterns of behavior, so that what we do within our imagination is of instinctual significance. It does affect the world, as alchemists, mystics, and Neoplatonists believed, but not quite in the magical way they believed. Because the images belong to the same continuum as instinct (and are not sublimations of it), archetypal images are parts of nature and not merely subjective fantasies "in the mind."

The figure of Pan both represents instinctual compulsion and offers the medium by which the compulsion can be modified through imagination. By working on imagination, we are taking part in nature. The method of this work, however, is not as simple as it might seem, for it is not merely an activity of the conscious mind or will, though they play their roles. The modification of compulsive behavior requires another psychic function, which we shall discuss below in regard to Pan's loves. First, we must look more closely at compulsion.

Already in the Orphic hymn (Taylor) we find compulsion in the description of Pan where he is twice given the epithet "fanatic," and in the Homeric hymn (Chapman) we can read that he climbs ever higher "and never rests." The same fanatic compulsion appears in the behavior attributed to him: panic, rape—and the nightmare.

The poles of sexuality and panic, which can instantly switch into each other or release each other, exhibit the most crassly compulsive extremes of attraction and repulsion. In the latter, we blindly flee helter-skelter; in the former, just as blindly we close upon the object with which we would copulate. Pan, as ruler of nature "in here," dominates sexual and panic reactions, and is located in these extremes. His self-division is presented in the Homeric hymn by his two "regions"—snowy, craggy mountaintops and soft valleys (and caves—and mythologically by the chasing phallic Pan and the fleeing panicked nymph. Both belong to the same archetypal pattern and are its nuclei. These two *foci* of Pan's behavior, representing the inherent ambivalence of instinct, also appear in his image, commented upon ever since Plato's *Cratylus* (408c), which is rude, rustic, and filthy below, smooth and spiritually horned above.

Yet, for all of his naturalness, Pan is a monster. He is a creature that does not exist in the natural world. His nature is altogether imaginal, so that we must understand instinct too as an imaginal force and not conceive it literalistically in the manner of natural science or of a psychology that would base itself upon science or metabiology. Paradoxically, the most natural drives are non-natural, and the most instinctually concrete of our experiences is imaginal. It is as if human existence, even at its basic vital level is a metaphor. If psychological behavior is metaphorical, then we must turn to the dominant metaphors of the psyche to understand its behavior. Therefore we may learn as much about the psychology of instinct by occupation with its archetypal images as by physiological, animal, and experimental research.

Panic

It might well be at this point to interpose something on the nature of fear. That it is a so-called primary affect has been stated by psychologists since St. Thomas and Descartes and is still confirmed by physiologists and by biologists specializing in animal behavior. Cannon has it as one of the four fundamental reactions that he investigated, and Lorenz regards it as one of the four basic drive complexes.

The traditional Western approach to fear is negative. In keeping with the attitudes of our heroic ego, fear, like many other affects and their images, is first of all regarded as a moral problem, to be overcome with courage as Emerson might say, or Tillich's "courage to be" in an "age of anxiety." Fear is to be met and managed by the hero on his path to manhood, and an encounter with fear plays a major part in initiation ceremonies. Because our culture's first reflection upon the psyche is habitually moral, the psychological value of fear tends to be prejudiced if not occluded from our perspectives altogether. So entrenched is the moral approach to psychological events that psychology has had to go to physiology and to the study of animals in order to find a path free of moralisms.

Although physiology recognizes the protective function of fear, the emotion of fear is generally regarded to be either an accompaniment of instinctual flight patterns or these same patterns blocked or retained within the organism. This inhibition of motoric behavior together with increased and prolonged excitation of the organism (vegetative nervous system and neuro-hormonal-chemical activation) is called "anxiety." Simply, there are two faces to panic: lived out in relation to a stimulus and called fear; held in with no known stimulus and called anxiety. Fear has an object; anxiety has none. There can be panicky fear, a stampede, say; there can be panicky anxiety as in a dream. In either condition death can result. Psychoanalytic and psychosomatic case reports, as well as dream research and anthropological studies (for instance, on Voodoo death) provide instances of the fatal consequences of panic.

The anxiety dream can be distinguished from the nightmare in the classical sense. The classical nightmare is a dreadful visitation by a demon who forcibly oppresses the dreamer into paralysis, cuts off his breath, and release comes through movement. The anxiety dream is less precise, in that there is no demon, no dyspnea, but there is the same inhibition of movement.[27] A literary prototype of the anxiety dream, emphasizing an inhibited peculiarity of movement, occurs in the *Iliad* (Achilles in pursuit of Hector):

> As in a dream a man is not able to follow one who runs from him,
> nor can the runner escape, nor the other pursue him, so he could
> not run him down in his speed, nor the other get clear.[28]

Some theorists of emotion would use the anxiety dream as evidence for their view that anxiety is inhibited fear, a flight pattern retained within the organism, as if instinct were divided into two pieces: action and emotion. During the anxiety dream, action being impeded, emotion intensifies. Anxiety, whether in dreams or not, remains in this rather positivist and behavioristic perspective a substitute, secondary, inadequate reaction. Could we take arms against the sea of troubles we would not be sicklied over.

Contemporary existential philosophy gives to anxiety, dread, or *Angst* a more intentional and oppressive interpretation. Angst reveals man's fundamental ontological situation, his connection with not-being, so that all fear is not just dread of death, but of the nothing on which all being is based. Fear thus becomes the reflection in consciousness of a universal reality.

Buddhism goes yet further: fear is more than a subjective, human phenomenon. All the world is in fear: trees, stones, everything. And the Buddha *is* the redeemer of the world from fear. Hence the significance of the *Abhaya mudrā* (of no-fear), which is not merely a sign of comfort but of total redemption of the world from its "fear and trembling," its thralldom to *Angst*. Buddha's perfected love, in the words of the Gospels, "driveth out fear."

To further mix the contexts: let us say that the world of nature, Pan's world, is in a continual state of subliminal panic just as it is in a continual state of subliminal sexual excitation. As the world is made by Eros, held together by that cosmogonic force and charged with the libidinal desire that is Pan—an archetypal vision most recently presented by Wilhelm Reich—so its other side, panic, recognized by the Buddha belongs to the same constellation. Again we come back to Pan and the two extremes of instinct.

Brinkmann [29] has already pointed to the bankruptcy of all theories of panic that attempt to deal with it sociologically, psychologically, or historically, and not in its own terms. The right terms, Brinkmann says, are mythological. We must follow the path cleared by Nietzsche whose investigation of kinds of consciousness and behavior through Apollo and Dionysus can be extended to Pan. Then panic will no longer be regarded as a physiological defense mechanism or an inadequate reaction or an *abaissment du niveau mental,* but will be seen as the right response to the numinous. The headlong flight then becomes a breakthrough, out of protected security into the "uncanny wilderness of elementary existence." Panic will always exist because it is rooted in human nature as such. So its management, Brinkmann says, must also follow a ritual, mythological procedure of gestures and music. (One is reminded of the pipes in battle and that Pan's instrument in many paintings is not a syrinx but more a trumpet.)

Roscher's enumeration of animal panics does indeed remove the discussion from the level of the only human and psychological in the narrow sense to more universal hypotheses such as offered by the existentialists, the Buddhists and the archetypal psychology exhibited in Pan. If we take the evidence that Roscher cites of Pan's terror to be a form of psychic infection attacking both man and animals, then we would seem to have an archetypal event that transcends the only human psyche, thereby placing the nightmare panic in a profound realm of instinctual experience which man shares at least with animals. With trees, stones, and the cosmos at large this sharing remains a speculation.

If panic in animals is not substantially different from panic in man and if panic is at the root of the nightmare, then the Jones nightmare hypothesis is not enough. For even the boldest Freudian has not extended the universality of the Oedipus complex and of repressed incest desire/ fear beyond the shepherd to the sheep. Freud's psychological hypotheses stop with the human world (even if his metapsychology of Eros does urge us into the direction we are here taking). Roscher, however, points beyond the human to a wider area of panic phenomena.

The Freud/Jones hypothesis explains the nightmare intrapsychically: repressed desire returns as demonic anxiety. But Roscher opens the way for a mythological perspective: the demon instigates both the desire and the anxiety. They do not convert into each other, owing to Freudian censors and the mechanical hydrostatics of libido-damming and dream-distorting according to the formula:

> The intensity of the fear is proportionate to the guilt of the repressed incestuous wishes that are striving for imaginary gratification, the physical counterpart of which is an orgasm—often provoked by involuntary masturbation. If the wish were not in a state of repression, there would be no fear, and the result would be a simple erotic dream.[30]

From this we are led to believe that the nightmare is unhealthy, the result of a faulty psyche. To put the matter in a Reichean parody of an older idea: perfect orgasm driveth out fear.

The view we are elaborating in this essay with its focus upon Pan and his role in the nightmare takes many of the same phenomena reported by Jones but sees them as evidence for another hypothesis. Anxiety is not a secondary result from subliminal sexuality; anxiety and desire are twin nuclei of the Pan archetype. Neither is primary. They are the sensuous qualifications of the more abstract poles of instinct, which moves between all-or-nothing, *accessum-recessum, Lust* and *Unlust.*

Jones himself brings supportive evidence for the idea that anxiety and sexuality appear together, which would seem to controvert his own formula. Like Roscher he refers to Börner:

> Sometimes voluptuous feelings are coupled with those of *Angst*; especially with women, who often believe that the night-fiend has copulated with them (as in the Witch trials). Men have analogous sensations from the pressure exerted on the genitals, mostly followed by seminal emission.[31]

> It is important in this connection to remember how frequent is a voluptuous trait in the *Angst* attacks of the waking state; indeed this often passes on to actual emission during the attack, a phenomenon to which attention was first drawn by Loewenfeld in the case of men, and by Janet in the case of women.[32]

Since the times of Jones and the authors he relies upon, there has been prodigious energy directed toward investigating correlations between physiological sexuality and dreaming. We know today from laboratory observation of human dreamers that penile erections come and go during sleep rather rhythmically following the curve of dreaming. But these investigations rather than making the understanding of the relation between sexuality and dreaming simpler have convinced us all that the field is more complex than it was envisioned by Jones and Freud. The relation between overt sexual content of a dream and the physiological sexual excitation (or its absence), the psychological and physiological subtleties of nocturnal emissions, the periodicity of sexual rhythm (both psychic and somatic), qualities of psychic sexuality in terms of specific archetypal constellations (e.g., whether the governing fantasy is Apollonic, Priapic, Narcissistic, and so on), the relation between the physiology of anxiety and the psychology of repression, more, what is repression and what is an "adequate" orgasm—these enigmas stand as mute as ever. They certainly are not resolved by psychodynamic simplifications which derive from theories that do not match the psyche in its complexity.

Anxiety and sexuality are words covering an immensely sophisticated range of experiences. Furthermore, these words cover experiences that are neither only actions or reactions, but are also metaphors for situations of consciousness governed by archetypal fantasies. In fact, the actions and reactions are themselves part of a metaphorical pattern and are meaningful within that pattern, expressing something always more sensuously qualified than what is covered by the definitions of anxiety and sexuality. One of these metaphorical patterns is provided by Pan. By placing anxiety, fear or panic against that background, we may not solve the dubious, if not nonsensical, "what is fear?" but we may gain insight into kinds of experience for which we use that word and thus make more precise the intentionality of fear.

Jung, in his *Seminar Notes,* discusses at times the problem of fear, finding it a legitimate path to follow. He seems to mean that one goes where one is afraid, not as the Hero in order only to meet the Dragon and overcome it. But fear as an instinctual pattern of behavior, as part of the "wisdom of the body" to use Cannon's phrase, provides a connection with nature (Pan) equal to hunger, sexuality, or aggression. Fear, like love, can become a call into consciousness; one meets the unconscious, the unknown, the numinous, and uncontrollable by keeping in touch with fear, which elevates the blind instinctual panic of the sheep into the knowing, cunning, fearful awe of the shepherd.

When Jung said that we need to learn to fear again, he picked up the thread from the Old Testament the beginning of wisdom is the fear of the Lord and gave it a new twist. Now the wisdom is that of the body that comes into connection with the divine, as panic with Pan, with the same intensity as described in the sexual visions of Saints. For where panic is, there too is Pan. When the soul panics, as in the story of Psyche's suicide, Pan reveals himself with the wisdom of nature. To be fearless, without anxieties, without dread, invulnerable to panic, would mean loss of instinct, loss of connection with Pan. The fearless have their shields; they have constructions preventing emergencies, the startle pattern held at bay by means of systematic defenses.

In other words, to borrow the formula style from Jones, panic and paranoia may show an inverse proportion. The more susceptible we are to instinctual panic, the less effective our paranoid systems. Further, as first corollary, the dissolution of any paranoid system will release panic. As second corollary, psychoanalytic statements about paranoia and the fear of homosexuality can be expanded beyond the erotic to include the implied other nucleus of the Pan archetype, panic. And, as third corollary, any complex that brings on panic has not been integrated into a construction and should not be. Therefore any complex that brings on panic is the *via regia* for dismantling paranoid defenses. This is the therapeutic way of fear. It leads out of the city walls and into open country, Pan's country.

Panic, especially at night when the citadel darkens and the heroic ego sleeps, is a *direct participation mystique* in nature, a fundamental, even ontological, experience of the world as alive and in dread. Objects become subjects; they move with life while one is oneself paralyzed with fear. When existence is experienced through instinctual levels of fear, aggression, hunger, or sexuality, images take on compelling life of their own. The imaginal is never more vivid than when we are connected with it instinctually. The world alive is, of course, animism. That this living world is divine and imaged by different gods with attributes and characteristics is polytheistic pantheism. That fear, dread, horror are natural is wisdom. Using Whitehead's term, "Nature Alive" means Pan, and panic flings open a door into this reality.

27. A collection of these dreams is given by M. Weidhorn, "The Anxiety Dream in Literature from Homer to Milton," *Studies in Philology* 64 (1967): 65–82.

28. *Iliad,* 22.199–201.

29. D. Brinkmann, "Neue Gesichtspunkte zur Psychologie der Panik," *Schweizerische Zeitschrift für Psychologie und ihre Anwendungen* 3 (1944): 3–15.

30. Jones, *On the Nightmare,* 343.

31. Ibid., 46.

32. Ibid., 49.

Pan and Masturbation

Roscher's article on Pan in the *Lexikon* states that Pan invented masturbation. Roscher refers to Ovid's *Amores* 1.5.1 and 26 and to Catullus 32.3 and 61.114. But the principal source is Dio Chrysostomus (ca. 40–112 CE), who in his sixth oration refers to Diogenes for witness. (Diogenes was the Greek Cynic philosopher who supposedly masturbated in public.)

A second, indirect connection between Pan and masturbation is brought out by Jones through an etymological analysis of *mare* (also discussed by Roscher), the "crusher" or oppressive night fiend retained in our word nightmare. Jones sees the meanings of the *MR* root to have "an unmistakable allusion to the act of masturbation."[33]

The sum of information we have on masturbation shows it to be historically and anthropologically a widespread practice. We know also that it occurs in certain higher animals (not only in captivity) and that it extends in the biography of a person from infancy into senility, that is, before other genital activities begin and often long after they have lapsed. In adults, masturbation runs parallel with so-called sexual behavior, never being a mere substitute for it. It is discovered spontaneously (by animals, infants, and small children); furthermore, it is the only sexual activity performed mostly alone.

When considering the relation between the mythical figure and the psychological act, let us first put aside the usual reductive simplifications, which attempt to explain the unknowns of a psycho-mythological association in terms of common sense. We are not dealing here merely with an eruptive sexual urge that occurs in solitude to hunters, fishers, warriors, herdsmen, and their lonely wives; we are not merely mythologizing what we fantasy about the sexual habits of shepherds during their noonday rest; nor is this association of Pan with masturbation another way of stating that the devilish inhuman goat in human nature will have its out no matter how. Rather the assignation of masturbation to pan is psychologically appropriate, even necessary, since masturbation provides a paradigm for those experiences we call instinctual, where compulsion and inhibition join. The psychology of masturbation makes more precise the ideas we touched upon above in regard to the two poles of instinctual behavior.

As I have elaborated elsewhere,[34] masturbation brings together two aspects of the instinctual spectrum: on the one hand, the urge; on the other, conscience and fantasy that accompany and divert the urge. We have long confused the shame that accompanies masturbation with a social prohibition, that is, with an internalized, censoring authority. We have long assumed that masturbation is wrong because it serves no extravertedly visible end. Biologically, it does not further procreation, so it must be "unnatural"; emotionally, it does not further relationships, so it must be "autoerotic"; and unloving; socially, it does not bring the libido into the social nexus, so it must be anomic, schizoid, suicidal even. Our usual views of it have been taken altogether from the standpoint of civilization, and so our understanding of its inhibition has come from the same standpoint. The introspective worry, guilt feelings, psychological conflict, in short, the *inhibiting* phenomena of conscience is considered to be merely the voice of a *prohibiting* authority, a super-ego.

The converse of this view tries to liberate masturbation from the restraining prohibition, freeing it to follow a Romantic's Pan in unbridled delight, neglecting the conscience factor and that the inhibition is *sui generis,* part of the compulsion itself, its other side. (Even hardened sexual offenders, that is, those imprisoned for rape, multiple child molestings, sadistic killings, report guilty feelings and troubled conscience about masturbation (!), according to the work of Kinsey's successors at the Indiana Institute. Guilt seems as inherent to masturbation as the compulsion itself.) The liberated approach to masturbation at least does not condemn it as psychologically regressive (appropriate for the young but not for adults). But this approach does make the activity psychologically meaningless. Deprived of its fantasy, shame and conflict, masturbation becomes nothing but physiology, an inborn release mechanism without significance for the soul.

This widely held notion and its physiological converse simplifies both masturbation and Pan. Both are a complexity of opposites in which the moment of inhibition is as strong as the compulsion. These opposites of Pan appear in the activity itself: either we retreat in fear from masturbating, pervaded by shame or frightening fantasies, or we shift from fear into courage by exciting our own genitals. Masturbation alleviates anxiety—as well as causing it, too, on another level. Fear of the evil eye was met, and is still met in some societies, by genital manipulations or at least genital signs. We ward off fear by touching sexuality, thereby propitiating Pan who invented masturbation and panic both. *Nota bene*: the sexuality that wards off fear is not coitus, i.e., connection with another, or even with an animal, but masturbation.

Furthermore, the fantasy factor appears in Pan as the configurations of his entourage, the exfoliation of nature, the water, caverns, and the noise of which he is fond (as well as his silence), his dance and music, his frenzy. The conscience factor manifests in hiding and retreat and in what our concepts call the "laws of nature," the rhythmical self-inhibition of sexuality. Human self-inhibition is less apparent than in animals whose sexual periodicity is clearly marked. Ours is more subtle, more psychic, and probably reflects first in fantasy and in the archetypal basis of conscience. Were the inhibition not there as an archetype, laid down in the same psychoid structure that is our sexuality, then whence the prohibitions concerning incest and rituals to regulate sexuality?

Therefore, when regarding masturbation, let us bear in mind its psychological significance. If psychological events have their bases in archetypal dominants, then behavior always has meaning, and the more archetypal (instinctual) the behavior, the more primordially significant it must be. To see the regression and not the significance is a blindness therapy may not allow itself. The psychology of the unconscious has established at least one axiom: meaning is in behavior itself. It is not given by consciousness to behavior. Acts we do that are regressively far from consciousness, like masturbation, may be serving other purposes than those of our conscious orientation. They may be senseless to our human mind and archetypally significant at the same time.

So we may regard masturbation to be governed by the goat-god of nature, who "invented" it, and as an expression of him. This mythological statement says that masturbation is an instinctual, natural activity invented by the goat for the shepherd. It says further that masturbation is significant and divinely sanctioned. Because it belongs to a god, the activity is mimetic to the god, conjuring him and summoning him in the concrete body. Masturbation is a way of enacting Pan.

Curiously, D.H. Lawrence did not see this. He was the closest to Pan of all the moderns,[35] and yet he also wrote strongly against masturbation. However the suppression of masturbation kills not only Pan as compulsion, but Pan's fantasy and Pan's shame, the inhibitory complications that accompany masturbation and are part and parcel of it. The suppression of masturbation as a physical act is also the suppression of its psychic counterparts. And when this suppression begins, the battle over masturbation becomes an interior theological dispute echoing the Judeo-Christian refusal and reformation of nature "in here." In our biblicized culture, let us remember, masturbation is attributed to Onan whom God struck dead, and not to Pan who was himself a god.

In sum: masturbation may be understood in its own right and from within its own archetypal pattern, condemned neither as substitute behavior for the lonely or isolated, as regressive behavior for adolescents, as recurrence of Oedipal fixations, nor as a senseless compulsion of physiology to be controlled by the opposite prohibitions of personal relations, religion and society. As masturbation connects us with Pan as goat, it also connects us with his other half, the *partie superieure* of the instinctual function: self-consciousness. Because it is the only sexual activity performed alone, we may not judge it solely in terms of its service to the species or to society. Rather than focusing upon its useless role in external civilization and procreation, we may reflect upon its usefulness for internal culture and creativity. By intensifying interiority with joy— and with conflict and shame—and by vivifying fantasy, masturbation, which has no purpose for species or society, yet brings genital pleasure, fantasy, and conflict to the individual as psychic subject. It sexualizes fantasy, brings body to mind, intensifies the experience of conscience and confirms the powerful reality of the introverted psyche—was it not invented for the solitary shepherd piping through the empty places of our inscapes and who reappears when we are thrown into solitude? By constellating Pan, masturbation brings nature's urgency and complexity back into the opus contra naturam of soul-making.

33. Jones, *On the Nightmare,* 332.

34. "Toward the Archetypal Model for the Masturbation Inhibition," in J. Hillman, *Loose Ends* (Dallas: Spring Publications, 1975).

35. See Merivale, *Pan the Goat-God.*

Rape

Like masturbation, rape is psychological behavior, and so it deserves psychological attention. Like masturbation and panic, it also exemplifies the relation between mythology and pathology, the theme at the heart of both this essay and Roscher's monograph. Part of the complex of rape is an emotional aversion to it; it is a violation, a transgression, a horror. An inquiry into this subject will therefore evoke the same aversion that is inherent to the archetypal pattern. The theme acts upon us itself as a rape, closing our subjectivity to it. Rape becomes a closed subject: what is there to discuss; it is what it is. Psychology would rather leave it criminalized, beyond the pale. Or, if it must turn to it, then by means of sophisticated conceptual avoidances, such as sadism, aggression, or revenge. One has to go outside psychology to literary minds Jean Genet, for instance) in order to find a readiness and an intelligence to look phenomenologically at rape.

To begin with: rape has belonged to human and divine existence long before psychology came on the scene to account for it. We therefore should not expect too much from psychology; its accounts have the puny tradition of only a few generations within the confines of a narrow culture, mainly Northern, Western, and Jewish-Protestant. Furthermore, besides the general inadequacy of psychology in dealing with the great archetypal themes, there is the specific *lacuna* in regard to rape, as if psychology's abstention from inquiry protects it from violation. (Other criminal acts and other sexual acts get far more attention.) Alexander Grinstein's five volumes[36] of forty-thousand entries give only four, and these peripheral, on rape. The classic view of psychoanalysis connects rape with infantile libidinal fantasies about a raping parent or an omnipotence fantasy about raping the parent. The Jungians have extended this with the idea of the phallic mother where sexuality is joined with aggression and imaged by the uroboric boar. I would like to dismiss this boring psychological tradition and make a fresh start.

If masturbation is "divinely sanctioned," invented by a god, then surely rape has even firmer ground in divinity since the rape of nymphs and of mortals—and of one god by another—is a convention of Greek mythology. Rape is not specific to Pan, yet it is characteristic of Pan and, as we shall see in the next section, it is his principal way with feminine figures, occasioning their flight and his frustration. (His raping attempts are not solely upon nymphs; there is Daphnis the shepherd boy, who, some tell, was attacked while taking music lessons from Pan, and there are the goats with which Pan copulates in various positions, shown by gem seals and statuaries.)

A Neoplatonist hermeneutic would say that rape of nymphs expresses the immediate, unreflected, and determined essence of divinity in the realm of natural affairs. Rape shows the compulsive necessity within and behind all generation. The closer one is to the world of material nature, the more sexual and compulsive will the divine power show itself. Rape is the paradigm for the divine penetration and fecundation of the resistant world of matter. Rapes in mythology may not be understood on a literal level, but should be perceived as theosophical allegory. Thus, Neoplatonism.

Now the "depravity" of myth, or what we refer to as its psychopathology, has long been a concern of exegetical readers. The apologists for antique religion had to contend with the charge of moral corruption thrown at them especially by the Christians (who, at least since Eusebius, saw the Devil in Pan). The Neoplatonist defense of myth was the most elaborate, consistent, and intellectual; its height of psychological understanding was reached in the Orphic philosophy of Renaissance Italy.[37]

Nevertheless Neoplatonism is a defense. It apologizes. It explains. Masturbation would not be really masturbation, but a symbolic expression for something else like self-generativity. Neoplatonism uses a hermeneutic method we are familiar with nowadays through Freud: the manifest is but a cover for a latent meaning that is more true and more real and more liberating than psychopathological (symptomatic) appearances. So with rape; this mode of exegesis does not accept *psychopathology as an essential mode of psychological life.* Yet this is precisely what myth says.

We may get a main point of the relation between mythology and pathology if we grasp that pathological behavior is mythical enactment, a *mimesis* of an archetypal pattern. After all, this is what Freud told us by "discovering" the Oedipus complex. He discovered that family psychopathology is the enactment of myth. In the case of rape, the archetypal pattern being enacted is a specific one that has been condemned by the other archetypes dominating our civilized consciousness, outlawing as renegade both Pan and rape.

The second main point about this relation reverses the first: mythology is necessarily pathological (descriptive of psychopathology), otherwise it could not speak about the actual soul. Then mythology would be purified, a kind of idealized religion (such as the German tradition has often tried to make of the Greek world, thereby paying a dreadful price in psychopathology). Mythology without its "moral depravities" would become a book religion, a humanistic construction or a revelation of ethical dogmas, and not the ongoing embodiment of human experience in which pathological patterns cannot help but be incorporated. So it seems myth includes rape as one of the events that must be portrayed by any system adequate to the true range of the soul.

Where then lies the difference between your or my raping and a raping by the figures of myth? If the myth explains (and sanctions) the pathology, then an imitatio Dei means rape too. Does the difference lie wholly within the context in which they are done? If we take this view, then we make a separation between holy and secular, and are back with the Neoplatonists. We would take the copulation of goats with women within an Egyptian temple (reported by Herodotus) on a sacred, ritual level. But does this help with the psychopathology of the rapist in the alleyway? Where are the contexts today for transposing archetypal enactments from secular to ritual?

To answer this, new forms of psychotherapy have been devised, and there are witch cults and sects, such as the one led by Aleister Crowley, that was dedicated to Pan and, according to Crowley's verse, included rape.[38] But they remain secular, since we cannot alone revive the gods. Pan must be present prior to the cult in his name. And thus these are not mythical enactments, but mythical constructions. In a sense there is truer myth being enacted in the alleyway than in Crowley's Sicilian temple or in a psychodramatic, Pan-dancing Californian workshop.

If not these external attempts, then perhaps the dream and fantasy and the imagination of the arts can transpose us to the mythical world where other laws obtain and where rape is "appropriate." This solution says that we may do whatever we want "in here," but not act it "out there." The sacred and mythical now become intra-psychic and mental, while the secular becomes behavior. This solution takes us back in another direction. This time we return to the Cartesian position and their radical separation between mind and matter. But it is the express aim of this essay to follow Pan by keeping "in here" and "out there" together, inseparable.

A fourth solution would say that what is pathology in the streets is also such in the mind. What we do in imagination has the same consequences for the soul as acting out. Now we are back in the Christian situation, where looking upon a woman with lust is the same and as sinful as external action. Fantasy is taken wholly literally.

Clearly the issue remains insoluble as long as we insist that behavior and fantasy are two different realms. This schism produces all the others: between secular and sacred, between "in here" and "out there," between mythology and pathology. Therefore the first step toward resolving the particular problem of rape is to recognize the larger mistake behind it. This mistake can be rectified by remembering that behavior is also fantasy and fantasy is also behavior, and always.

This means, first, that fantasy is also physical; it is a mode of being in the world. We cannot be in the physical world without at the same time and all the time demonstrating an archetypal pattern. We cannot move or speak or feel without enacting a fantasy. Our fantasies are not only in the mind; we are behaving them.

Second, the union of fantasy and behavior means that there is no pure, no objective behavior as such. Behavior may never be taken on its own level, literally. It is always guided by imaginal processes and expresses them. Behavior is always metaphorical and requires a hermeneutic approach as much as does the most fantastic reverie of mystical vision.

These observations may relieve the term "psychopathology" from having to serve two masters, the legitimate one of psychology and the parasitical one of morality. Moral criteria of behavior belong to ethics, law, and religion, but these fields should not influence the perspectives of psychopathology, whose judgments concerning behavior are determined less by what, where and with whom actions take place than how. Less the act than its quality.

We become *more* psychopathological when we miss, in this or that segment of our lives, the fantasy in an act or that what we are fantasying is physically happening, even if subtly and indirectly. Instead we literalize, and metaphor that keeps life psychologically intact breaks apart. When metaphors no longer hold, we have, on the one hand, literalized fantasy in hallucinations and delusions; on the other, literalized behavior called psychopathy or behavior disorder of which rape is sometimes considered a symptom.

We become *less* psychopathological when we can restore the metaphorical appreciation of what is going on. Therapy speaks of "psychological insight," which would mean the reconnection of fantasy with behavior, and the dissolution of literalism through the power of insight. Because law, ethics, and religion tend to take behavior with the same literalism that psychology regards as the origin of psychopathology, these fields must not encroach on ours—more, their judgments arise from the same psychopathological literalism as the behavior they judge. (I have already expressed this necessary conflict between psychology and these other fields in regard to suicide, where my emphasis too was upon the metaphorical perspective to behavior.)

So psychology is obliged to consider rape always as metaphorical, even yours and mine, even in the street. This premise is already a therapeutic act for it affirms the unity of fantasy and behavior. Even in the street there is always ritual taking place in behavior and something transhuman is always going on in everything profane. The transposition we have been searching for is a transposition in our vision of things, a psychological transposition so that we can see the unity of fantasy and behavior. Then we do not need to construct literal enactments and call them rituals. This essay is just such an attempt at the transposition of our vision. By seeing Pan in panic, masturbation, and rape, we restore both the god to life and life to the god.

Without this vision of the god in behavior, rape becomes only psychopathology. As I showed in earlier works, when we lose sight of Eros in analysis, transference erotics become only neurosis; without Saturn and Dionysus, depression and hysteria become only psychiatric diagnoses. We lose sight that, though syndromes are sufferings, they belong to a wider pattern. In each of these situations the modern mind has tended to see the pathology before the psychology, forgetting that the sickness is a part of significance. The *pathos* is part of *psyche* and has its *logos*. The pathological—however drivenly distorted and concretistic—nevertheless belongs to soul-making. This the Neoplatonists recognized. They saw that since the mythical stories had meanings for the soul, so did all the parts of the stories, including their bizarre depravities, the horrors which are imaginatively essential to the stories, but which today we call psychopathological.

Let us keep in mind that the archetypal horror of rape affects even this discussion of it. The best witness to the effects of the archetypal horror is the legal suppression of rape. In the United States, generally, neither does a seminal emission nor actual penetration of the vagina or anus belong to its definition. Forced juxtaposition of the genitals is enough to bring down the power of the judiciary. More: there is a purely legal (statutory) rape, such as congress with a consenting minor, a genital examination by a physician, or a general anesthetic by a dentist (with no third party present). These are not trivialities. The death penalty for rape, including statutory rape, still exists in some parts of the United States. This displacement of horror into nonsexual, legal niceties belongs to a long tradition of suppression going back to Colonial times. In Pennsylvania, for instance, Blacks already in 1700 were castrated for attempted rape (of whites).

Let us place the horror of rape within the constellation of Pan. First of all, Pan goes after nymphs, that is, rape aims at a form of indefinite consciousness located still in nature but not personally embodied. This consciousness is still only-natural, just as Pan's drive is only natural. The nymph is still attached to woods, waters, caves, wispy figments, mistiness; she is chaste, nature still intact, a maiden (see below, "Pan's Nymphs").

Pan brings body, goat-body. He forces the sexual reality of physical generation upon a structure of consciousness that has no personal physical life, whose life is all "out there" in impersonal nature. Pan's assault suddenly turns nature into instinct. Rape makes it intimate. Rape brings it "in here" from "out there." The impersonal enters from below into the very private body, bringing an awareness of the impersonal as a personal experience. As such, rape is a horror because it is an archetypal transgression. It forcibly crosses between two unrelated structures of consciousness, whose distance from each other is stated in the language of opposites: old woman/young man, young girl/old man, virgin/lecher, white/black, native/foreigner, old inmate/young punk, soldier/civilian, master/slave, beauty/beast, upper class/lower-class, barbarian/bourgeois. But this transgression is also a connection between these structures. Rape puts the body's drive toward soul into a concrete metaphor. It presses the soul into concreteness. It forcibly ends the division between behavior and fantasy, violating the soul's privileged distance to live life through reflection and fantasy.

To interpret the transgression rape as aggression is archetypally wrong. Aggression is insignificant in the constellation of Pan. He does not beat or throttle the obscure objects of desire; no gun or knife-blade belong to his threat. Pan's rape, like Pan's nightmare, is a close encounter with the animal force of the body. His assaults and our rapes mimetic to them are not aggressions; they are compulsions. They are not so much attacks to destroy the object as they are a clutching need to possess it.

The language of rape usually speaks of deflowering, the paradigm for which is Persephone picking flowers when seized by Hades. Deflowering too must be taken metaphorically for we are not speaking of the hymen rupture of actual virgins, but of flower consciousness broken through and its death. How few actual rapes are of actual virgins, yet in fantasy all are virgins, whether sisters, daughters or nuns, whether young boys, schoolgirls, or old maids, or freshly jailed first-time "offenders." The fantasy of defloration and virginity appears together with rape. Empirically this association makes little sense; psychodynamically it is a secondary elaboration and not essential. But, archetypally, the association of rape and virginity is necessary for it shows that the behavior is ruled by the fantasy of Pan and the nymphs. On the one hand, the untouched, a consciousness without bodily senses; on the other hand, the toucher, the touching sensuous body. Touch, contact, connection-this is crucial to the metaphor which so dwells on body language. Pan, who is sometimes called the invisible, is nonetheless envisioned most physically as raper. He is called jumping, bold, barbarous, ferocious, rough, unwashed, hairy, black Pan. These epithets in Latin were given to Pan.[39]

The fear of the Black and primitive raper existed in Western consciousness long before Pennsylvania was founded. If, as is said, a sexual fear is the psychological source of the repression of Black people, and if Pan has been imagined as *niger, instabilis, lubricus, rusticus, brutus, nudus, nocturnus,* etc., then is not one archetypal source of our racist social ills the loss of Pan, so that he becomes utterly unconscious and collectively projected. The law has incorporated the nymph-Pan fantasy by formulating protective concern for nymphets and for anesthetized women and by projecting the rapist into the touch of the examining physician. Legally, rape is necessarily neither coitus nor ejaculation. These essentials of the sexual act do not define rape legally. Even the law recognizes in a sinister way that rape is something over and beyond actual sexuality. The true transgression is the connection on the genital level between two structures of human existence that have different ontological status.

Pan the raper is a potential within every sexual impulse. Every erection may release him, implying a need for psychic deflowering. As psychologists we must first see this fact before we accuse it or defend it. Some necessity of the psyche can convert an impulse into a rape fantasy, or even produce a rape fantasy without sexual arousal. There is an attempt at transgression going on, an attempt to move across from one level to another, bringing sex and death to a part of the soul that is altogether resistant to this kind of awareness.

Euripides describes a rape as a "panic marriage."[40] Pan grabs, seizes, couples. The violence compares with the nightmare demon whose visit is unbidden, covers the sleeper, stopping the breath that cuts the victim off from the airy element, pneuma. Despite the panic, the coupling is nonetheless a "marriage," a uniting of fates. The fateful encounter is hardly a human marriage of persons, for this union joins a monstrous impulse with wounded innocence.

Pan the raper will be conjured up by those virginal aspects of consciousness that are not physically real, that are "out of touch," unsensed. Feelings and thoughts that remain wispy and flighty, that still are cool, remote, reflective will call rape upon them. They will be assaulted again and again by concretisms. Pure reflections will be raped again and again in order to bring them into behavior.

The raper chasing the virgin is another way of putting behavior in search of fantasy to cool its compulsion. The loathing of the virgin is another way of putting fantasy's fear of physical behavior. But the virgin's violation is inevitable whenever the boundaries are drawn too tight between fantasies too removed from body and fantasies wholly immersed in body. Then the concrete metaphor of "forced genital juxtaposition" is constellated re-uniting fantasy and behavior.

The psychodynamic idea of compensation would express this idea by saying that the concrete bears in on one—as rape, panic, or nightmare—when consciousness is too ethereal, ephemeral. The concrete compensates for distance from physical life, which is represented in concentrated paradigm by the genitals. But psychodynamics, while trying to put events back into the psyche, gets them back only into the ego. These horrors (rape, panic, nightmare) are said to happen because the ego is doing something wrong. The inrush of the numinous power becomes only a psychic mechanism to correct the ego. Explanations in terms of compensation forget that the experience is altogether trans-psychological. It comes as the numinous. Pan's arrival is uncaused, *sui generis*. He irrupts.

Yet this emphasis on the concrete in psychodynamics has importance if we take it phenomenologically, letting go of the theory of balancing opposites. Phenomenologically, rape, panic, and nightmare embarrass consciousness with concreteness, and thus always strike us as psychopathological: the events are so literal. Again, the psychopathology resides not in what happens but in the how, the concrete metaphor of the happening. Rape, panic, and nightmare belong where anxiety and sexuality are taken so concretely that the psyche has already become a victim, caught, oppressed, its freedom lost. The horror has already begun.

From the perspective of the nymph's consciousness rape will always be horror. This horror, too, is archetypally authentic and therefore this horror is significative and not merely a prissy resistance and a symptom of anxiety. Horror warns. It tries to keep a structure of consciousness intact. Reflective consciousness is in danger of being overwhelmed (*vergewaltigt* = rape in German) and violated (*viol* = rape in French) by the very physical world that it reflects. Reflective consciousness turns away. This is its natural movement, for reflection too is instinctual (see below, "Pan's Nymphs"). To keep its reflective structure untrammeled, this aspect of consciousness must not let the nightmare that is nature get on top of it and cover it. Nature's nightmare side is the suffocating oppressive concretism expressed by the epithets of Pan and in the experience of Ephialtes.

But—concretism occurs in every literal question we put to someone, in every thrust of hard-headed advice, every penetrating interpretation about how to live and what to do. We rape and are raped not only sexually. The sexual is but a metaphor for moving "from belong" (reductively) into someone's personal intimacy in a crude and "only natural" manner. Nothing constellates these transgressions across the border more than do innocent questions from the simplistic nymphic mind.

Concretism obscures the light and blocks the movement of fantasy. From this perspective, defloration means not penetration and transformation but a broken soul. From this perspective a pure spark of reflective light must be kept intact at all costs. A spontaneous insight gives the freedom to move away from nature's oppression and igniting the capacity to imagine life and not only to be driven by it.

36. A. Grinstein, *Index of Psychoanalytic Writings* (New York: International Universities Press, 1960).

37. See "Pan and Proteus," in E. Wind, *Pagan Mysteries in the Renaissance* (Harmondsworth: Penguin, 1967), and also Taylor's translation of Proclus's "An Apology for the Fables of Homer," in *Thomas Taylor the Platonist,* for two easily accessible works explaining this approach.

38. See Merivale, *Pan the Goat-God,* 122ff.

39. J.B. Carter, *Epitheta deorum quae apud poetas latinos leguntur,* in *Ausführliches Lexikon,* Supplement (1904).

40. Euripides, *Helen,* 190.

Pan's Nymphs

By placing instinct and image on the same continuum, Jung offered a new entry to Pan's world. Rational, moral, and willful attempts to manage instinctual compulsions can only suppress instinct, since these attempts arise from an essentially different component of the psyche. Likes connect with likes; likes cure likes. Mythical images depict instinct; instincts enact mythical patterns. (Vico thought myths were therapeutic.) Logically and practically, Pan's urges are best approached via his companionate mythical images: his nymphs.

In this respect myth can be compared with alchemy. In alchemy the transformation of compulsive sulfur requires a substance equal to it (mainly salt, but also and by means of mercury, an evasive psychic substance that is the true instrument of change). The operator's mind and will play a role subsidiary to the effects of one substance upon another. So, too, in the changes represented by myth, a mythologem equal to Pan is required.

Before we go further, I must qualify the idea of change in myth by hastening to add that we are not engaged in moral instruction. There is nothing "wrong" with Pan, with instinct, compulsion, and the like. Myths describe fundamental subjective subjective processes in which changes are embedded. It is our mistake to read these changes as moral improvements, as progresses of any sort. Thus to speak of the "cure" of compulsion is, on the one hand, a therapeutic notion implying betterment; but, on the other hand, "cure" means the change from one form of affliction into another. Let us keep distinct the core notion of change from its interpretative coatings: some sugary as "growth" and "progress," some more bitter as "loss" and "decay." If an axiom of psychic change is like cures like, we can hardly bring about change on one level by doing things on another. Of course, sulfur and salt are opposites, and cure comes, as Heraclitus would have enjoyed remarking, through the opposites. But the opposites are within the same class and at the same level.

Thus a change of compulsion is not a matter of consciousness working on the unconscious, for these are opposites of two different classes, similar to will working on imagination, super-ego working on id, or mind working on body. Mind may work on mind, body on body; and so to change events of an imaginal nature, we shall be obliged to stay within an imaginal field.

Furthermore, for change to take place at an instinctual level, the process must be natural; it must be as the alchemists said: nature both loving and enjoying nature and at the same time nature changing nature. The opposites must be already sames, and there must be an affinity between them. In alchemy, *sol* loves *luna,* and fire and water embrace. In mythology, Pan wants nymphs. We have seen that Pan divides between mountaintop and grotto, between noise and music, between hairy thighs and spiritual horns, between headlong panic and headstrong rape. Another instance, and one more imaginative and appealing, is Pan and his partners, the nymphs. For a god and his partner describe the two main components of an archetypal complex. And if the noblest truth of psychological thinking (Jung) as well as of mythical and mystical philosophy[41] is the identity of the opposites, then not only are the twin nuclei within Pan's nature one and the same, but also Pan and the nymphs are necessarily entailed because they too are one and the same. "The nymphs who accompany Pan are not his subordinates…they remain just as divine as he is," writes Philippe Borgeaud.[42]

Roscher's etymological and "natural" explanation of nymphs[43] takes them as personifications of the wisps and clouds of mist clinging to valleys, mountain sides and water sources, veiling the waters and dancing over them. And indeed Homer[44] says that is where the nymphs live. In the same volume, Bloch[45] refuses Roscher's hypothesis by saying that the word in Greek mythology means nothing else than "mature maiden" or "miss," corning from swelling as does a bud, and rather like our "nubile," but not "nebulous." W. F. Otto, in his chapter on the nymphs,[46] agrees that the word means girl or bride, but connects them mythically first of all with Artemis and the Greek feeling of *Aidos,* shame, a modest bashfulness, a quiet respectful awe within nature and toward nature. He describes this feeling as the opposite pole to the overwhelming convulsiveness of Pan (god of epilepsy). The nymphs belong to the same inscape of our interior nature as does Pan.[47]

Who are these nymphs of myth, these loves of Pan? First of all, many had no names; these "impersons" bespeak on the level of the drive-object the impersonality of the drive. The same invisible unspecific power instigates Pan's rapes as objectifies them in the unknown obscure nymph. Of those named, there is Syrinx, a water maiden who, fleeing his sexual assault, transformed into a reed from which Pan made his pipes. Although perhaps the most famous of all his loves, Syrinx is given secondary attention by scholars because the tale is said to be a late mythologizing explanation for Pan's pipes. Before considering the tale of Syrinx and its dismissal by scholarship, let us allow the nymphs to pass in review.

Pitys, a nymph of the pine tree, was another. Pan often wears a pine wreath or a chaplet made of fir, and the pine cone occurs often together with Dionysus, its pointed shape and its many seeds allowing it to be called that favorite interpretative euphemism of Victorian Classicists, a "fertility symbol."

But here Pitys, the pine, is feminine, and reflects Dionysus in another way, for the mixture of pine and wine in *retsina* expresses a *coniunctio*. D.H. Lawrence amplified Pitys in his own fashion, experiencing Pan in and through the pine, its "bristling," pungent roughness. For Lawrence the pine is less the comforting shade on a hill slope of Roscher's fantasy evoking the wood-nymph of bucolic Greece, than the aggressive maleness of the Red Indian in Lawrence's work "Pan in America." The pine tree as Pan, as male, restates the Orphic thesis that the opposites are identical, Pan and the nymphs are one. There are, for instance, statues of female Pans and there are pictures and reliefs where Pan appears together with a hermaphrodite.[48]

A third of Pan's loves was Echo, whom we have met in Apuleius's tale of Eros and Psyche. Here, too, Pan was frustrated, for Echo had no body, no substantial existence of her own. In relationship with Pan she was altogether he himself resumed upon himself, a repercussion of nature reflecting itself. (In the case of Narcissus, whom Echo loved, it is Narcissus who refuses her for the allure of his own reflection.)

Reflection seems the aim as we proceed further through the list of Pan's loves. For another was Eupheme, wet nurse to the Muses. She and Pan had a boy together, named Crotus, who, as the Muses' half-brother, used to play with them. Eupheme's name means "spoken fair," "good repute," "religious silence." From that root we have "euphemism," which means the propitious use of words.

Harsh or unlucky events can be modified if given a better name. The right use of euphemism nourishes the Muses. It lies at the source of the transformation of nature into art. Absurd or crude misfortunes of nature may be shaped by imagination. As Pan can turn rout and riot into dance, clamor into music, so his nightmare force seeks better (euphemistic) expression that gives his harshness and crudity a further significance, a more poetic and religious value. The relation of Pan with Eupheme and the Muses also implies that within all the arts there lies, covered over, the primal evocative power of Pan.

Finally, the one who fully reveals Pan's intention is Selene, goddess of the moon. (Her entire configuration and her son Musaeus and his connections with Orpheus and with the Eleusinian Mysteries are implicated by the Pan-Selene story, but to take them up would require a separate monograph on Selene, which Roscher, by the way, also accomplished.) However, we must note these characteristics of Selene: her unsurpassed beauty, her eye that saw all things happening below; her rule of menstruation, the orderly rhythm of female instinct; her gift of dew, the cooling moisture; her relation with epilepsy and healing; the veil that kept her partly hidden, indirect; the torch she carried and the light-bestowing *diadem* she wore; the obscure cave from which she rose and in which she set.

For his conquest of the moon, it is said that Pan had to disguise his black and hairy parts with white fleece. This is the language of alchemy, corresponding to the movement from *nigredo* to the *albedo* of lunar consciousness. What is resistant to light, obscure and driven, suffering nature in ignorance, turns white and reflective, able to see what is going on in the night. The white fleece does not halt Pan in the course of his conquest. The whitening is not an *askēsis* of the goat. It is not that Pan now knows and so does not act out, but the action, by becoming white, turns reflective and thus the connection with Selene (*selas* = light, like that of a torch shining in the night) has been made possible. Like cures like: Pan, by becoming like Selene is already connected with her.

Nor does this tale say that Selene's lunar consciousness reflected Pan and thus deflected him. To the contrary, the seduction takes place. Lunar consciousness can be swept away by a Pan; it can be convulsed and can panic, faint, and collapse.[49] The lunar state is particularly vulnerable to Pan, just as Pan is particularly attracted to it. This we have already seen above in regard to rape. Here, it is reaffirmed, for Pan makes his most vivid impression as Ephialtes in dreams which traditionally belong to the Moon. And there in nightmares his lunatic nature appears especially. Pan was one of the gods directly associated with lunacy, as the nymphs were a cause of madness (nympholeptoi).

We are now in a position to return to Syrinx. Though this tale may be a late invention, a mere consciously literary conceit, its pattern is authenticated by its similarity with the other tales. It is as if the mythologist's invention was preformed by the archetype of Pan and the nymph to tell us in one more version the relationship between Pan, frustration and reflection. Because a tale is late does not mean it has lesser psychological insight or mythical value. Archetypal primordiality must not be confused with historical antiquity. In the Syrinx tale Pan pursues the possibility of reflection, which, by ever-receding, transforms into its instrument. The music of the Syrinx is the self-consciousness that inhibits and transforms the compulsion. Instead of rape on the riverbank, there is plaintive piping, song, and dance. The compulsion is not sublimated, however, but expressed in and through another image, for song and dance are also instinctual. Through the syrinx the noise Pan is fond of becomes music, the tumult, a measured step; patterns elaborate; there is space, distance and air, like the soughing of the wind in the pine. Like Echo, who provides the feminine receptivity of the ear and of recalling, the music made through Pan's pipes offers a musing fantasy that inhibits compulsion. Pan's sexual compulsion seems wholly directed towards the end of reflection. Remember: Pan is not a father god, his offspring being mythologically insignificant. His generative is of another sort.

These tales tell us that instinctual nature itself desires figures and fantasies to make it aware of itself. No new principle is introduced, no corrective of compulsion from above or outside the configuration of Pan himself. He seeks an intangible other pole—a mere reed, a sound, an echo, the pale light, the muse's nurse—a helpful awareness through the dark of concretistic sexuality and panic. Pan tells us that the strongest longing of nature "in here" (and maybe "out there" as well) is towards union with soul in awareness, an idea we have already seen prefigured in masturbation and conscience. The "other" whom Pan chases so compulsively is none other than his own nature, his own soul, reflected, transposed to another key.

The key is music. Sound. Syrinx, Echo, and Pitys—who sighs (Nonnus) or moans when the wind blows through the pine trees are the sounds of nature. The nymphs reflect nature to the ear. They teach listening, and listening stops compulsion. If Pan contains an elemental kind of reflection, then we should expect to find reflection also in his own imagery and exemplified not only in the nymphs. And this we do find. Besides the music and dance, there are his shielding protective activities. Besides the Nike link with Athene—having Penelope for a mother and/or Ulysses for a father, as told by some traditions, implicates Athene—there is the fathering seed of Hermes (or Zeus, Apollo, Cronus, Uranus, Aether, or Ulysses, each of whom presents a mode of reflective spirit). Moreover there is the motif of his early rising, his appearance on vase paintings together with the dawn, the breakthrough of day.

More significant perhaps than any of these images of reflective consciousness is the fact that Pan appears in the representations of art again and again as an observer.[50] There he stands, or sits or leans or crouches, amidst events in which he does not participate but where he is instead a subjective factor of vital attention. Wernicke says he serves to waken the interest of the onlooker, as if when we look at a painting with Pan in its background, we are the observing Pan.

Pan the observer is shown us most strikingly in those images of him with his hand raised to his forehead, gazing into the distance: Pan the "far-seeing," the "sharp-eyed," the herdsman above the herd, on guard, watching. Within the physical intensity of Pan there is a physical attentiveness, a goat's consciousness. The consciousness is not Olympian, because it is not an embodiment of superior detachment. His reflection is in connection with the herd, the awareness identical with the physical signals of nature "in here." The reflection is *in* the erection, *in* the fear, an awareness that is nature bound, as are the nymphs to their trees and rivulets, blind yet intuitive, farseeing yet immediate. Pan reflects altogether in the body, the body as instrument, as when we dance, and for which Lawrence used the metaphor of the Red Indian. This is a consciousness moving warily in the wisdom of fear through the empty places of our inscapes, where we do not know which way to take, no trail, our judging only by means of the senses, never losing touch with the flock of wayward complexes, the small fears and small excitations.

This body consciousness is of the head, but out of the head, lunatic, more like the spirit in the horns. (And the moon has horns.) It is not mental and figuring out; it is a reflection, but neither after nor even during the event (in the manner of Athene). Rather it is the manner in which an act is carried through, appropriate, economical, a dance style. As Pan is one with the nymphs, so his reflection is one with behavior itself. Rather than an epistemic subject who knows, there is the animal faith of *pistis*, surefooted like a goat.

The path of Pan can still be "Let nature be your guide," even where wild nature "out there" is vanishing. Nature "in here" can nevertheless be followed even through the cities and domestications, for the body still says "yes" or "no," "not this way, that," "wait," "run," "let go," or "move in now and have it."

What more could we wish from prophecy than this immediate body awareness of how, when, and what to do. Why ask for grand visions of redeemers and the fall of civilizations; why expect prophecy to come with a long beard and thunderous voice. That is too easy, the pronouncements too loud and clear. The prophet is also an interior figure, a function of the microcosm, and thus prophecy may sound no stronger than an intuition of fear or a jet of desire.

Plutarch placed his story about the death of Pan in a discussion about why the oracles had become defunct. With the death of Pan, the maidens who spoke out the natural truths were no more either, for the death of Pan means as well the death of nymphs. As Pan eventually turned into a Christian devil, so the nymphs became witches, and prophecy became sorcery. Pan's messages in the body became calls from the devil; any nymph who evoked such calls could be nothing but a seductive witch.

Pan's kind of consciousness is inherently mantic, from the ground up, so to speak. (We shall return to this theme in the next section.) It was from Pan that Apollo learned the art before he took over Delphi from Themis.[51] The nymphs excite to a madness, both to nympholepsy and to the prophetic gift. The nymph Erato was prophetic at Pan's Arcadian oracle, and Daphnis, the name of Pan's shepherd love, was *promantis* at the oldest of all Delphic oracles, that of Gaia.[52] The list is long of those turned mad by nymphs or gifted by them with mantle powers.

Pan and the nymphs therefore played their part in a special kind of mantics, those that healed.[53] The waters and places beneficial for physical restoration had their *spiritus loci,* usually a nymph. According to Bloch, the nymphs brought about healing, madness and prophecy by their effects upon fantasy. As Otto says,[54] the nymphs are preformations of the muses. The nymphs excite imagination, and one still turns to nature (instinctual in here or visible out there) to kindle imagination.

There is no access to the mind of nature without connection to the natural mind of the nymph. But when nymph has become witch and nature a dead objective field, then we have a natural science without a natural mind. Science devises other methods for divining nature's mind, and the nymph factor becomes an irregular variable to be excluded. Psychologists then speak of the anima problem of the scientist. But the nymph continues to operate in our psyches. When we make magic of nature, believe in natural health cures and become nebulously sentimental about pollution and conservation, attach ourselves to special trees, nooks, and scenes, listen for meanings in the wind and turn to oracles for comfort—then the nymph is doing her thing.

The archetypal nymph continues to appear in the findings of clinical research into nightmare prone people. Ernest Hartmann's work at Tufts University[55] concludes that nightmare sufferers are "people whose sense of boundary is soft and undefined. They find it difficult to keep fantasy and reality separate…They do not have a firm, clear idea of their own identity." Furthermore, Wernick reports a curious little study showing that "art majors were three times more likely to have nightmares as were physical education majors." Again, Pan and the Muses.

The nymph in the modem soul has made the modern cult of Pan; if Pan lived vividly in the literary imagination, especially of the nineteenth century, then so did the nymph. That recrudescence of Pan may be seen altogether as a product of the nymphic imagination, an anima style of consciousness that hovered in nubile not-yetness and horror of sexuality, in fainting, in the neurasthenic retreats into the vegetative nervous system of the misty Victorian England of Elizabeth Barrett Browning. Her first rapture on Pan was written when she was herself a nymphet of eleven or twelve.[56] Another encounter of a Victorian with the nymph can be read in Clifford Allen's paper on John Ruskin.[57]

In every nymph there is a Pan, in every Pan a nymph. Rawness and shyness go together. We cannot be touched by Pan without at the same time fleeing from him and reflecting upon him. Our reflections about our impersonal, filthy, gross sexuality, and our delight in it, are echoes in us of the nymph. The nymph still makes us feel shocked, and lascivious. And when goaty feelings and fantasies break out in the midst of daydreams, Pan has again been evoked by a nymph.

In each of the stories of Pan and the nymphs, including the one of his birth—for Dryope, his mother in the Homeric hymn, was a wood nymph—the nymph flees in panic from Pan. Now Pan is not the only one to make nymphs flee. Flight is essential to nymphic behavior. Think of the chases of Zeus and Apollo and Hermes. So we must ask what is going on here; what does this archetypal pattern of flight signify? Since "all of the gods are within" and since myth is going on all the time at the archetypal level of our existence, then this flight of the nymph is also going on as a process in the backwoods of the soul.

Let us put together Pan's compulsions (panic and rape) with the feminine object of his compulsion. Let us recapitulate the relation between instinct and inhibition. It was believed that Pan himself was in panic when the animals ran, and that this vision of Pan's panic set the world in terror. It is as if Pan was himself a victim of nightmares, epileptoid convulsions, and the horror that he brings. The god is what he does; his appearance is his essence. In one and the same nature is both the power of nature and the fear of that power.

In our discussion of panic we said that fear is a call to consciousness. The nymphs show this fear in their panicked flight. They are thus showing one of nature's ways, flight, which is one of the four primary instinctual reactions described by ethnologist Konrad Lorenz. Psychologically, flight becomes reflection (*reflexio*), the bending backward and away from the stimulus and receiving it indirectly through the light of the mind. As Jung says about this instinct:

> *Reflexio* is a turning inwards, with the result that, instead of an instinctive action, there ensues a succession of derivative contents or states which may be termed reflection or deliberation. Thus in place of the compulsive act there appears a certain degree of freedom...
>
> The richness of the human psyche and its essential character are probably determined by this reflective instinct. Reflection reenacts the process of excitation and carries the stimulus over into a series of images which, if the impetus is strong enough, are reproduced in some form of expression. This may take place directly, for instance in speech, *or may appear in the form of abstract thought, dramatic* representation, or ethical conduct; or again, in a scientific achievement or a work of art.

> Through the reflective instinct, the stimulus is more or less
> wholly transformed into a psychic content, that is, it becomes an
> experience: a natural process is transformed into a conscious con-
> tent. Reflection is the cultural instinct *par excellence*...[58]

Here, Jung has conceptualized the archetypal mytheme of Pan's chase
and the nymph's flight. Jung's conceptual theory is another way of stating the fantasy of the tales of the fleeing nymph. In both we find the
transformation of nature into reflection, into speech, art, and culture
(Eupheme and the Muses). The base of this transformation is the power
of images released by the flight reaction. In a sense, culture begins in
Pan's compulsion and the flight from him.

But lest we give too much to reflection—for alone it is sterile[59]—let us
keep reflection close to its prototype, fear. There consciousness and culture are instinctually rooted. When reflection is rooted in fear, we reflect
in order to survive. It is no longer just mental reverie or contemplative
knowledge.

By emphasizing the importance of the fear-flight-reflection complex
we are deliberately diminishing the usual major role of love in creating
culture. Eros does not seek reflection in the same compulsive way as Pan.
Rather, love would abjure reflection that impedes its course; love would
be blind. Even when its aim is Psyche as in the Apuleius tale, there is a
distinct difference between Eros and Dionysus, on the one hand, and
Pan, on the other. Their similarities are evident and their clustering
(together with Aphrodite and Ariadne, with satyrs and *silenoi,* rabbits
and kids, pine, wine, ivy, etc.) in mythical and allegorical representations
is familiar enough. The differences are less familiar.

For one thing, Pan is active, the nymphs passive; the maenads are
active to Dionysus's sombre quietness. For another, Eros is not a nature
figure as much as he is a *daimon.* He is often winged with unpronounced
genitals, whereas Pan is often a goat with an erection. The metaphor of
Eros is less concrete, physical; his intentions and emotions are different
in quality and physical locus. In contrast to Pan's chases, there are no
stories as such (excepting that told by Apuleius) of his loves. He is usually
the *agens,* not the agonist. In both Eros and Dionysus, psychic consciousness seems to be present and active (maenads, Psyche, Ariadne), but in
Pan instinct is always in search of soul.

A way of looking at this cluster is to follow the tradition which places
both Eros and Pan in the train of Dionysus, as subsidiaries of that cosmos.

A long tradition of wall and vase paintings shows Eros and Pan wrestling, to the amusement of the Dionysian circle.[60] The contrast between the clean stripling Eros and the hirsute awkwardness of rustic paunchy Pan, with victory to Eros, was moralized to show the betterment of love to sex, refinement to rape, feeling to passion. Moreover, the victory of Eros over Pan could be philosophically allegorized to mean "Love conquers all."

This opposition I see also in terms of love versus panic, but not in the Christian sense of love overcoming fear. The issue here is not who conquers whom and the morals that can be derived from this victory. Rather the issue is the contention between the way of Pan and the way of love. The death of Pan supposedly coincided with the rise of love (the Christ cult). Perhaps, the recognition of Pan as a psychic dominant implies a lessening of the tributes we pay to love, whether as Eros, Christ, or Aphrodite.

Love plays no part in Pan's world of panic, masturbation, rape, or in his chase of nymphs. These are not love stories; these are not tales of feelings and human relationships. The dance is ritual, not a couple moving together; the music sounds the uncanny pipes of Mediterranean tones, not a love song. We are out of the cosmos of Eros altogether, and instead there is sexuality and fear. Perhaps this explains why our civilization has such trouble with masturbation and rape. They could not be fitted into a world of love. When judged from love's perspective, they become pathological.

We must then draw the conclusion that the realm of love does not include all the instinctual factors of human nature, just as the figure Eros is only one god among many. Eros does not provide appropriate guiding images for areas of our behavior governed by Pan. To go on judging our Pan behavior in the light of love continues a suppression of instinctual qualities and an enmity towards nature that cannot but have psychopathological results. The struggle between Eros and Pan, and Eros's victory, continue to put Pan down each time we say a nightmare is a bad dream, rape violates relatedness, masturbation is inferior to intercourse, love better than fear, the goat uglier than the hare.

Certainly rape is more violent, the nightmare more dreadful, masturbation more solitary, and the goat more smelly than the usual harmonies of civilized domestication. But phenomena that disrupt the usual are not *ipso facto* morally repugnant. If all things are full of gods, as

Euripides is said to have said, then all things have their divine backing and are governed by Necessity. Even the Bible says: "To every thing there is a season, and a time to every desire under heaven."[61] Moral judgments made inside the walls of civilization and the laws protecting the citizen cannot do justice to outsider phenomena whose range is often "way out." The pulpit must condemn and the law incarcerate the rapist, but the psychologist's task is different. We must try to see phenomena in their own right, bracketing out our civilized commitments. The psychologist has one foot outside the wall.

Finally, the insights drawn from the relation of Pan and the nymphs can correct the Christian idea of Pan as god of unbridled pagan sexuality to be controlled by Judeo-Christian prohibitions whether through love or law. If the nymphs and Pan are one, then no prohibition is necessary. An inhibition is already present in the compulsion itself. Thus, sexual passion is both holy and one aspect of reflection, as Lawrence insisted. Animal desire brings with it its own shame, its own piety.

> ...in composite gods the tension between chastity and passion, or penitence and pleasure, which is generally associated with the conflict between Christianity and paganism, was revealed as a phase of paganism itself.[62]

41. E. Wind, "Pan and Proteus."

42. Borgeaud, *The Cult of Pan in Ancient Greece*, 173.

43. "Pan," *Ausführliches Lexikon*, 3.1:1392ff.

44. *Odyssey*, 6.123.

45. L. Bloch "Die Nymphen," *Ausführliches Lexikon*, 3.1:500ff.

46. W. F. Otto, *Die Musen und der göttliche Ursprung des Singens und Sagens* (Darmstadt: Wissenschaftliche Buchgesellschaft, 1954).

47. Concerning the interior nymph, its attractiveness and its dangers, see E. Jung, "The Anima as an Elemental Being," in *Animus and Anima: Two Papers* (Putnam, Conn.: Spring Publications, 2008); also *CW* 13:179ff., 215ff.

48. K. Wernicke on Pan in art, in *Ausführliches Lexikon*, 3.1:1406ff.

49. Also belonging to Pan, according to E.R. Dodds, *The Greeks and the Irrational* (Berkeley and Los Angeles: University of California Press, 1951).

50. Wernicke, op cit., lists three columns of examples.

51. Bloch, "Die Nymphen."

52. Pausanias, 10.5.5.

53. See below Roscher's evidence on Pan and healing dreams.

54. Op. cit. sup. on the nymphs and the Muses.

55. R. Wernick, "Hartmann," *Smithsonian Magazine* (August 1989), http://www.robertwernick.com/articles/nightmares.shtml. Accessed September 2, 2014.

56. Merivale, *Pan the Goat-God,* 81.

57. C. Allan, "The Problem of John Ruskin: A psychosexological analysis," *International Journal of Sexology* 4.1 (August 1950): 7–14.

58. *CW* 8: 241–43.

59. See my *The Myth of Analysis: Three Essays in Archetypal Psychology* (Evanston, Ill.: Northwestern University Press, 1972), Part I.

60. Wernicke, op. cit., 1457, and Herbig, op. cit., 32.

61. Ecclesiastes 3: 1.

62. Wind, "Pan and Proteus," 204.

Ecology

A question from Pan might ask us: "Why are you civilized people who profess compassionate Christianity so hard on the environment? Why do you blast, bulldoze, and flatten so many acres of scrub woodlands and hillsides? Why are there fewer and fewer lonely places where people may hide in nature and nature hide from people? Are you trying to eradicate my haunts? Put a final solution to the problem of Pan?"

Pan might go on to say: "Sometimes I believe you practice a reverse psychology, a psychology of projection. You rape nature and call me the rapist. You serve your own private desires and call me the masturbator. You leave tracts of ruin, yet claim I am the god who favors deserted wilderness. Is not your dayworld becoming a suffocating nightmare? Your children having more and more trouble breathing? Are you not security obsessed, seat-belted against surprise, medicated against panic attacks? And what have you done to save the nymphs, the tiny differentiated sounds of nature, nature's little night music? Parks, resorts, golf courses, and well-marked trails—no nymphs there, no risk of swooning at the earth's beauty. No risk of panic either."

To answer Pan let us imagine that science and its engineering technology is deliberately persecuting Pan, not merely to rid society's progress of fuzzy mystical nature-thinking. But more importantly science fears the return to Pan "in here." Since Pan is Ephialtes and the nightmare, he is unpredictable and amoral.

His urges live in the barren places of the psyche where the mind of civil engineering makes no inroads. He hides in the psyche's caves, the soul's wilderness. His promptings to rape, to masturbate, to take flight in panic are alive in the most well-regulated civilian. Is not a basic cause of contemporary environmental devastation "out here" a continuation of Western history's determination to keep control "in here" over the most potent and enduring of the ancient gods, to ensure that the great god Pan stays dead?

Little wonder that environmentalists receive little sympathy. Beneath the scorn these tree huggers evoke and the violence they sometimes suffer is fear of Pan. Environmentalists serve not only the proud, isolated goddess Artemis in her duty to protect the wild world and its animals. Devotees of nature are also servants of Pan, therapists of his cult, as the world *therapeia* first means—worshiper, servant, devotee of a god or a cult.

So it is not surprising that one-time Secretary of the Interior Watt of Utah and Congresswoman Chenowith of Idaho should both on different occasions declare that environmentalism is paganism. The return to nature invites Pan, and should the great god Pan and his Paganism be alive, then what does this imply for Christianism? The fearful righteousness of the two officers of the state perceived the god in the ecological calling; they saw its dangers and they gave warning to environmentalists that following Pan is a dangerous path because civilized Christianity wants him dead.

But let us not restrict the wild world to a bucolic Arcadia placed now in the empty areas of Utah and Idaho. The city, too, has its lonely spots and dark caves. It excites libidinous spontaneity. Goatiness inhabits the urban scene, hangs on to street corners, and, like, Ephialtes, visits nightmares on the most urbane of city dwellers. The wild may not be confined to wilderness as imagined in the usual opposition between sublime nature and degenerate city. "Wild" can be freed from natural wilderness, and wilderness itself be de-literalized so that Pan can return to the city.

Athens, the model of all cities, had its Pan cult. Lucian called Pan *summachos,* or ally of Athens, where he had his sanctuaries and rituals. According to Borgeaud,[63] Pan balanced the militarism of Athene and Ares by his favoring music and dance, laughter, mystery rites, and an alliance with "the smiling one," Aphrodite. Arcadia appears in the guise of the romantic city, misty, languid, nostalgic, evocative—Paris, Manhattan, Venice, Dresden—Pan's syrinx becomes saxophone, Selene becomes moony longings, the city a haunt of nymphs and nympholepsy.

63. Borgeaud, *The Cult of Pan in Ancient Greece*, 133ff.

Spontaneity – Synchronicity

Pan's hour was always noon. At this moment he would appear in the blaze and shimmer of midday, startling man and animal into blind terror. This seems to have little to do with the nightmare. Perhaps we need to regard high noon, the zenith of the day, as the highest point of natural strength, which constellates both the life force and its opposite, the necessary fall from this height. It is the uncanny moment when I and my shadow are one. Noon, like midnight, is a moment of transition and, like midnight, daybreak, and sunset, a radix of primordial orientation for what might be called the symbolic clock. These are the moments when time stands still, when the orderly procession of moments disrupts. So certain things must be accomplished before the cock's crow at dawn, or at the stroke of midnight, or before night falls. At these moments time is broken through by something extraordinary, something beyond the usual order. The *Mittagsfrauen* appear, or ghosts at midnight—compare Nietzsche's vision of the eternal at noon in his *Thus Spake Zarathustra*. This is the moment when the moment itself matters, where the moment is severed from before and after, a law to itself, a quality, altogether a constellation of the forces in the air, without continuity and so without connection to "…the waste sad time/Stretching before and after."[64]

This is the unrelatedness of Pan, and of the spontaneous aspect of nature. It simply is as it is, at where it is at; not the result of events, not with an eye to their outcome; headlong, heedless, brutal, and direct, whether in terror or desire. This is what is meant by the spontaneity of instinct—all life at the moment of propagation or all death in the panic of the herd. We may read into this behavior many explanations. We may find spontaneity "caused" by deeper laws of self-preservation and the survival of the species. We may see a larger ecological pattern to lie behind these sudden events, that they belong to a wider network of interwoven complexity. We may consider quantum jumps and the principle of discontinuity to be operative in humans and animals (and not only in inorganic physics). Or, we may conceptualize spontaneity in terms of inborn genetic codes being released within an inborn time cycle. Still the spontaneous frolic of kids, the gambol of lambs, as well as, the erection of the shepherd or his uncanny fright occur as instantaneous unconnected events. Spontaneity remains outside explanation. By definition it cannot be accounted for.

Spontaneity means self-generating, non-predictable, non-repeatable. It does not belong within the domains of natural science as science is defined, although it does seem to be a natural phenomenon. To find laws of the spontaneous would be a contradiction in terms, for these events are irregular, lawless. Thus to consider spontaneous events as random events that can be charted in Fisher's tables blurs the categories between quantity and quality. Random is a quantitative concept; spontaneous is qualitative and significative, pointing to what Whitehead called "importance." There is emotion with spontaneity. It means radically free.

By considering Pan to be the background for spontaneity,[65] we are suggesting an approach to spontaneous events by means of archetypal psychology. We look for the principle that governs them, their archetypal dominant, so as to imagine them more psychologically, and also to understand more psychologically the tradition of difficulty in comprehending and conceiving such events. Pan will not explain them, but he may offer an avenue of insight.

The spontaneous panic out of noon's stillness reappears in another configuration, the *Kobold,* or little demon, also said by Roscher to cause panic and nightmare. This being, too, has a sexual connotation: it is phallic, dwarf-like, fertile, both lucky and fearful. Herbert Silberer (probably Freud's most talented and adventurous pupil whose depth of psychological insight into alchemy, active imagination, and dreams did not save him from suicide) took up the *Kobold* in relation to "accidental" events. His work is one of the first psychological investigations into the archetypal background of chance, or so-called uncaused phenomena.

Silberer attributed chance events to the spontaneous appearance of these *Kobold* figures. They may be taken as a kind of *Augenblicksgott,* in the language of Hermann Usener. Or, they may be imagined like the daimon that suddenly cautioned Socrates, or any "personification" of a self-willed event that works like an entity crossing our path. Jung considered these events partly as psychic complexes, partly as spirit demons.[66] Above all, he gave them full recognition as authentic to nature.

Today we use concepts for these experiences, concepts like hunch, intuition, uncanny feeling, or even prophecy, in the sense we mentioned above. And parapsychology speaks of a sixth sense, which humankind shares with animals. These concepts do not take us very far. We are still left with the feeling assumption that there is a level of awareness, distributed wherever there is instinctual life and which echoes this life in sudden signals.

Myth has put this idea as the dismemberment of Echo. In Longus's tale of Daphnis and Chloe, Echo was torn apart by Pan's herdsmen (for refusing him). Her singing members were flung in all directions. Let us say that Pan speaks in these echoing bits of information which present nature's own awareness of itself in moments of spontaneity. Why they occur at this moment and not that, why they are so often fragmentary, trivial, and even false—these questions would have to be explored through the mythology of the spontaneous rather than through either empirical or logical methods. We would have to penetrate further into the nature of Pan (and the nymphs) in order to fathom these manifestations that seem to want to remain renegade and wispy, half-pranks and half-truths, and so bound to strong emotions. But the approach to their irregularity would be hermeneutic rather than only systematic. Jung worked both systematically and hermeneutically upon chance events as evidence for his hypothesis of synchronicity. This term refers to meaningful coincidences of psychic and physical events for which no satisfactory account can be given through the usual categories of causality, space, and time. Jung considered synchronicity to be a principle equal to the other three and, like them, a part of nature. He found that sudden, irrational, peculiar, yet meaningful connections happen mainly when instinctual (emotional, archetypal, symbolic) levels of the psyche are engaged. Pan cannot be identified with all emotion, with all of the archetypes. But when a meaningful coincidence occurs that has a particularly sexual cast, or starts up a panic, or refers to his time (noon and nightmare), or his landscape, and attributes, or the mood of his nymphs, then we should look to him for insight. But even more than this, Pan may play a role in synchronicity in general, since Pan like synchronicity connects nature "in here" with it "out there." Again Jung's conceptual fantasy of synchronicity and the imaginary fantasy of Pan have a common reference.

If the principle of synchronicity is another way of speaking about Pan, then we may also begin to understand why anyone occupied with this field of spontaneity, called parapsychology, becomes a renegade from the civilized order of rational men. As synchronicity is the devilish fourth principle, so Pan is the devilish shadow of our dominant archetypal Trinity. The integration of parapsychology into respectable science and psychology would then require a revaluation of Pan and a view of instinct and nature from his perspective. Until then parapsychology will tend to be cast in his shadow, a field of sentimentalities and natural religion, something at once comic, untrustworthy, obscure and lunatic—much as our rational civilized mind still views Pan.

64. T.S. Eliot, "Burnt Norton," V.
65. Cf. Matthew Arnold's essay "Culture and Anarchy."
66. *CW* 8:570–600.

Healing Our Madness

The god who brings madness can also take it from us. Like cures like. Yet how little attention has been given to Pan in all the writings on mental illness. Pan was one of the few figures in Greek mythology to whom mental disease was directly attributed.[67] We read from Roscher that Soranus considered Pan responsible for both mania and epilepsy, which we might delimit with the language of today by saying that Pan (*inflator*) rules our hypomanic states, especially those with sexual compulsions and hypermotor activity, and he rules sudden seizures that convulse the whole person, whether panics, anxieties, nightmares, mantles (speaking with tongues).

Using the psychoid, genetic metaphor, Pan would rule at the deepest level of our frenzy and our fear. At the same time Pan heals at this level, and there are connections between Pan and Asclepius through the attributes of music, phallus, nightmare vision and mantle insight. Both Pan and Asclepius heal by means of dreams. Through the nymphs special localities heal and bless. We have also seen Pan help the despairing Psyche; similarly, he frees the captured Chloe in Longus's tale.

Perhaps now we should read again Plato's prayer to Pan quoted as a motto to this essay. The prayer is said by Socrates in a dialogue whose main concern (much disputed) is the right manner of speaking about eros and madness. The dialogue ends with Pan as it opens on the shady banks of a river near a place sacred to nymphs. Socrates reclines there, barefoot. There at the beginning Socrates mentions that he is still struggling with the maxim "know thyself" and with his sense of ignorance about his true nature.

Then at the end comes the prayer with its appeal for inner beauty, which would mean an end to ignorance, for in Platonic psychology insight into the true nature of things brings about true beauty. Pan, then, is that god able to bestow the special sort of awareness that Socrates needs. It is as if Pan is the answer to the Apollonic question about self-knowledge.

What is this awareness and how is it achieved? We have seen that Pan is god of both nature "in here" and nature "out there." As such Pan is the bridging configuration who keeps reflections from falling into disconnected halves where they become the dilemma of a nature without soul and a soul without nature, objective matter out there and subjective mental processes in here. Pan and the nymphs keep nature and psyche together. They say that instinctual events reflect in soul; they say that soul is instinctual.

All education, all religion, all therapy that does not recognize the identity of soul with instinct as presented by Pan, preferring either side to the other, insults Pan and will not heal. We can do nothing for the soul without recognizing it as nature "in here" and we can do nothing for instinct without remembering it has its own fantasy, reflection, and psychic intentions. The identity of the twin nuclei of Pan, whether as behavior and fantasy, compulsion and inhibition, sexuality and panic, or the god and his nymphs, means psyche and instinct are inseparable in every moment. What we do to our instinct, we also do to our souls.

This idea, if taken in the full reaches of the mythological motifs and behaviour of Pan, has consequences. It means that selfknowledge recognizes the presence of Pan in the obscurest caverns of the psyche and that he belongs to it. It means further that self-knowledge recognizes that Pan's "horror" and his "moral depravities" also belong to the soul. This insight, by giving the goat its due, may bring the beauty for which Socrates prays. And by recognizing Pan so completely Pan may provide the blessing Socrates seeks, where inward and outward are one.

Socrates's prayer to Pan is even more relevant today. We will not be able to find our way back to harmony with nature through the study of it alone. Though today's major concern is ecological, ecology as such is not enough. The importance of technology and scientific knowledge for protecting nature's processes goes without saying, but part of the ecological field is human nature, in whose psyche the archetypes dominate. If Pan is suppressed there, nature and instinct will go astray no matter how we strain on rational levels to set things right. In order to restore, conserve, and promote nature "out there," nature "in here" must also be restored, conserved, and promoted to precisely the same degree. Otherwise our perceptions of nature out there, our actions upon it, and our reactions to it, will continue to show the same mangled exaggerations of inadequate instinct as in the past. Without Pan our good intentions to rectify past mistakes will only perpetrate them in other forms.

The re-education of the citizen in relation to nature goes deeper than the nymph consciousness of awe and gentleness. Respect for life is not enough, and even love puts Pan down, so that the citizen cannot be re-educated through ways which are familiar. These all start with Pan dead. The re-education would have to begin at least partly from Pan's point of view, for after all it is his natural world that we are so worried about. But Pan's world includes masturbation, rape, panic, convulsions, and nightmares. The re-education of the citizen in relation to nature means nothing less than a new relationship with these "horrors," "moral depravities," and "madnesses" that are part of the instinctual life of the citizen's soul.

If Pan brings the madness, then he is its healer. Like cures like. He belongs in the education of the citizen. As master of instinctual soul, he has something to teach about rhythms and range. Pan was a music man and called a great dancer. He made his appearance felt in choral gatherings, in the beat of rhythmic clapping,[68] bringing communal order to private panic. Music carries the body out of its separated loneliness. It educates (lit. "leads out") the soul driven into itself by fear. It has been claimed that dance styles begin in the animal world; humans learned motions and gestures from animals, the ballet masters of ritualized spontaneity. Dance comes from out of the wild, and its intoxication leads us back into it.

Strictly biblical societies have been horrified by dance. Awhile back it was polkas and waltz, then foxtrot and charleston, then dirty imports—tango, rumba, lambada. Dance had to be chaperoned, denounced, forbidden. The horror of dance is the horror of Pan; Hebraism versus Hellenism, control versus spontaneity.

If the society suffers the disease of wild rapaciousness, masturbatory exhibitionism, eruptive violence, and loss of an intimate sense of nature in the supposed "emptiness" of a "lost generation," their wilderness and their wildness, then the god in the disease is Pan. He offers an education in music that compels that generation—music within the halls of education, not merely exploitive commercialism. Then Pan returns from noisy cacophony to syrinx and flute, lightstepping intricacy of the goat-footed god. Then we might see that it is not Pan who is mad and must be healed, but the society that has forgotten how to dance with him.

This leads us back to the nightmare and the revelation through it of the horrifying side of instinctual soul. Socrates's puzzlings upon himself at the opening of the *Phaedrus* (230*a*) have a similar focus. He considers his likeness to Typhon, a demonic giant of volcanic eruptions, storms and underground earthquakes, "the personification of nature's destructive power."[69] To "know thyself" in the *Phaedrus* begins with insight into nature's demonic aspect.

The nightmare reveals this. There the healing re-education might begin because there instinctual soul is most real. Jones reminds us that "the vividness of Nightmares far transcends that of ordinary dreams."[70] Roscher and Laistner observed this, and Jones quotes others who have stressed this reality:

> The degree of consciousness during a paroxysm of Nightmare is so much greater than ever happens in a dream...Indeed I know no way which a man has of convincing himself that the vision which has occurred during a paroxysm of Nightmare is not real.[71]

> The illusions which occur are perhaps the most extraordinary phenomena of nightmare; and so strongly are they often impressed upon the mind, that, even on waking, we find it impossible not to believe them real.[72]

From this kind of experience Jones draws his main point condensed into the second motto I placed at the opening of this essay: the vividness of the nightmare experience pas given rise to the belief in the objective reality of personified demons and gods or nightmare as experiential base of religion. Of course for Jones, there are personal psychosexual dynamisms, so that the fertile power of his insight into the relation between the nightmare and the reality of the gods is gelded by the theory to which he yokes it.

The horror and the healing effect of the nightmare takes place not because it is a revelation of sexuality as such, but of the fundamental nature of the human being who as sexual being is at one with animal being, with instinct, and thus at one with nature. Pan's vision of our humanity is that we, too, are pure nature in whom the volcanic eruptions, the destructive seizures and typhoons also reside. This reality cannot be borne home in abstract concepts. Nature's metaphor is concrete and shaped. It must be felt, sensed, visioned in the actual, very real experience of hair and hooves. We must be paralyzed and suffocated by this reality as if there were something euphemistic in consciousness that always is in flight from "the horror." This sense experience was once, and still is, the vision of Pan in his nightmare forms. Thus Roscher, Laistner, and Jones in different ways are right in finding significance in the nightmare. Its numinous power requires a commensurately overwhelming idea: through the nightmare the reality of the natural god is revealed.

67. Dodds, *The Greeks and the Irrational,* 79 with note; cf. G. Rosen, Madness in Society (London: Routledge, 1968), 77ff.

68. Phillippe Borgeaud, *The Cult of Pan in Ancient Greece,* 150.

69. Schmidt, "Typhoeus, Typhon," *Ausführliches Lexikon,* vol. 5:1426.

70. Jones, *On the Nightmare,* 71.

71. J. Waller, in ibid.

72. R. Macnish, in ibid.

PART TWO

Ephialtes

A PATHOLOGICAL-MYTHOLOGICAL
TREATISE ON THE NIGHTMARE
IN CLASSICAL ANTIQUITY

Wilhelm Heinrich Roscher

*On the Psychological Importance
of the Text and Its Author*

by James Hillman

The following monograph is a classic example of nineteenth-century European scholarship. Here we can follow a significant problem—both for scholarship and for life—amplified and analyzed by a man of massive learning. This monograph is also an example of neglected learning. Like a prehistoric creature, the bulk and complexity of its appendages made it not viable for translation into another time and culture, so that it has remained an unread relic preserved in the bogs of academic libraries and only referred to in footnotes as a preformation of later works. Inasmuch as my "Essay on Pan" is one of those later works depending upon his research, it is appropriate to honor that text and the man who wrote it.

Owing to the fact that Roscher's monograph was written in a more leisurely age when the cost of printing detailed footnotes in Greek was not as inhibiting as it is now, scholars would liberally back up any statement made in a text with a wealth of quotes in Greek of similar examples. Sometimes this ostentation went beyond the useful, becoming more a mannerism, which academic publications still at times affect. In preparing this translation it was necessary first to choose between the essential and the merely curious. The ideal choice, to include every note in literal exactitude, was no real choice at all since it would have meant abandoning the project altogether. Instead we decided to print an accurate translation of the text with ample notes, so that the nonspecialist reader in English might profit from an essential work, yet without the exorbitant footnote apparatus supplied by Roscher. Those footnotes that are relevant have been mainly woven into the body of the text, which has been faithfully and completely rendered into English. The reader is thus not obliged to move the eyes both horizontally across the page and vertically up and down between footnotes and text. For this same reason, easier reading, all Greek terms have been transliterated into familiar letters, even in the third chapter, which is an etymological investigation. A "Bibliographical Endnote" describes the layout of the original monograph as well as giving bibliographical information.

Anyone with enough expert knowledge to follow the matter beyond what is given here would of course also be able to pursue that interest directly to the original—not only the German of Roscher but the Greek on which Roscher's work is based. Therefore this translation is less for the philologist than it is for us whose wider interest in dreams, myths, and the terrors of the soul is cramped by the contemporary malaise of "little Latin and less Greek." We need not thereby be cut off totally from knowledge of antiquity, and so this translation aims to reconnect us to that tradition but in our own language.

Wilhelm Heinrich Roscher was the son of the famous German economist Georg Friedrich Wilhelm Roscher, who receives more space in the biographical dictionaries than does his son. Roscher senior was one of the founders of the historical school of political economy, which played its part in the development of modern Germany under Bismarck. Roscher junior was born in Göttingen, February 12, 1845, and the family moved to Leipzig three years later. He was educated there at the Nikolai Gymnasium and the Sächsisches Landesgymnasium Sankt Afra near Meissen, moving on to study classics for three semesters at Göttingen, receiving his doctorate back in Leipzig in 1869.

During the second half of the nineteenth century, Leipzig was a major focus of German scientific and scholarly activity. It was important not only for its economic expansion, but it grew also as a publishing center and as the scene of new architectural achievements, including its famous art museum. Robert Schumann and Richard Wagner had studied in Leipzig, as did Ivan Pavlov later; Theodor Mommsen held a chair, while in the medical sciences, there was Wilhelm His in anatomy, Paul Flechsig in brain research, Adolf von Strümpell in neurology, and Carl Reinhold August Wunderlich, a reformer of German medicine and the man to whom we owe the foundations of clinical thermometry. Wilhelm Ostwald's work in physical chemistry took place in Leipzig, which was also where Gustav Theodor Fechner had his laboratory. Psychophysics can be said to begin with Fechner, as experimental psychology begins with Wilhelm Maximilian Wundt, who founded his institute in Leipzig in 1878, which soon became the desired sanctuary of American graduate students in psychology.

This was Leipzig, intellectual background of Roscher's youth and midlife, and he too was a pioneer investigator and indefatigable assembler of data in the nineteenth-century style. It is only now that we can see his achievements in scholarship as equaling those of his contemporaries in the natural sciences. He more than any other classicist is responsible for having collected into one place the mythical and religious material of the ancient world, providing the ground for the scientific study of myth and symbol. Among his fellows at the University of Leipzig were Friedrich Nietzsche and Erwin Rohde, the classicist known to us perhaps best for his work *Psyche, or the Cult of Souls*. With them Roscher founded the Philology Club. Roscher and Rohde traveled together to Italy, and Roscher visited Greece and Asia Minor in 1873–74. In 1876, he married Marie Eveline Henriette Koller who, according to Roscher's obituary in the *Neue Zürcher Zeitung*, was a Swiss from Herisau. They had three children. Roscher's only son (again a Wilhelm) and his son-in-law served on the Western Front during the 1914–18 war, and Roscher found in his research solace from anxiety over them and the war, which his father had long before predicted. He is said to have had a quiet and contained nature, working into old age at his table as long as the daylight lasted.

His external career was entirely as an educationalist. He taught Classics at his old high school, Sankt Afra, for eleven years, and then taught at the *Gymnasium* at Wurzen until he was sixty. He rose through various ranks in the secondary school system: *Oberlehrer, Oberstudienrat, Konrektor, Rektor, Geheimrat*. The benefit of all his learning went to pupils in the equivalent of the Senior High School. This points to a difference between the selective Continental and the democratic American notions of education. It also points to a difference regarding the role of the Classics between the end of the last century and the latter part of this. Roscher lived another eighteen years after retirement, dying at seventy-eight in Dresden on March 9, 1923.

Roscher devoted the major part of his scholarly life to the *Ausführliches Lexikon der griechischen und römischen Mythologie* (The Comprehensive Dictionary of Greek and Roman Mythology). Publication began in 1884, and it had been completed under Roscher's editorship through the letter "T" when he died. Each of his eight volumes contains about sixteen hundred columns of small print, which, if reset today would give us at least twelve thousand pages. Yet, the articles—not each authored by Roscher, even if all under his supervision—are written almost in a shorthand, abbreviating, and condensing everything possible. The *Lexikon* surveys not only the entire corpus of the Classical authors but reviews the later literature, makes comparisons, offers comments, and as well is richly illustrated, for Roscher was completely familiar with the art, architecture, and archaeological finds relevant to his subject. The work is still basic and still valuable; a recent printing of it, as completed by other hands, in ten volumes, has been reproduced photomechanically by Olms of Hildesheim. It continues to provide the stuff for countless articles on mythology today, and the *Lexikon* is standard in footnote apparatus. Most of his earlier researches and those done contemporary with the production of the *Lexikon—Apollon und Mars* (1873), *Juno und Hera* (1875), *Hermes der Windgott* (1878), *Die Gorgone und Verwandtes* (1879), *Nektar und Ambrosia* (1878), *Selene und Verwandtes* (1890) as well as his works on Pan—were integrated into the larger *Lexikon*.

As the titles indicate, he was particularly interested in comparative mythology, which in his later works extended beyond the Greek and Roman sources. So we find, for instance, in this study on the nightmare that Roscher turns to Byzantine works, psychological studies of his day on sleep and dreams, and expands upon material from other mythologies and lore of Northern Europe and Asia. In 1897, he examined the role of dog and wolf in the eschatology of the Greeks, trying to discover connections between religious ideas of these animals in antiquity and the problem of the werewolf, cynanthropy, and lycanthropy. He published on these subjects before this monograph on the nightmare appeared in 1900, when he was fifty-five years old. Later he became fascinated with more abstract topics: numbers in Greek medicine; the numbers seven, nine, and forty; and the concept of an imaginary middle point, the *omphalos* or navel of the world—a recurrent theme in Greek, Roman, and Semitic mythology. He published also on these subjects. We can see a biographical pattern in his writings that move from a study of the separate archetypal personifications of the gods through an interest in the more terrifying psychological forces (nightmare, sexuality, werewolf, lycanthropy) to subjects typical for senex consciousness when Saturn tends to rule, e.g., numbers and the idea of the center.

But Roscher was more than a compiler and encyclopedist. His mind sought out unusual aspects of his subjects, going beyond the historical and philological. His scholarship was, in a way, touched by the Romantic currents that flowed through late nineteenth-century rationalism, warming it and breeding within it surprising new kinds of life, the most important of which was the psychology of the unconscious. Roscher's work in mythology belongs as much to the sources of depth psychology as does the work of Edward Burnett Tylor, James George Frazer, and other early anthropologists, or the work of Jacob and Wilhelm Grimm and the folklorists, or in another line, Roscher's contemporaries in the medical field: Jean-Martin Charcot, Hippolyte Bernheim, and Sigmund Freud. The exploration of the background of the rational mind, whether through the disciplined instigation of hysterical dissociation, of the thought habits of "primitive" peoples, or of the beliefs of the past through linguistic, mythological, or archaeological investigation, all culminated in what is today the psychology of the unconscious. Jung's concept of the archetype rests on the evidence accumulated by these different disciplines.

If we see only one of the intertwined roots of C.G. Jung's work—for example, Freud or Paul Eugen Bleuler, or the basis in Wundtian association experiments, or the early interest in parapsychology and occultism, or the problems of Christian theology and its heresies (alchemy)—we are likely to miss many other aspects of the background to modern depth psychology. Moreover, since modern depth psychology was emerging by means of these new nineteenth-century disciplines (psychiatry, anthropology, folklore, spiritualism, comparative religion, and mythology), we must read the history of these fields also from the psychological point of view. They did not describe in their hypotheses and their findings merely material from their respective fields; they were as well speaking of what was soon to be called "the psychology of the unconscious."

Therefore, these pioneer works provide not only the historical background for their modern descendants in "scientific" psychiatry, anthropology, and mythology, they as well contain a psychological ferment, swelling many of their hypotheses preposterously beyond what today would be allowed by the "facts." We thus may not blame Roscher for the wide casting of his net nor for some of the odd fish he comes up with. Classical studies of this century have put tight critical restrictions upon nineteenth-century scholarship, questioning its method and evidence, its Eurocentric bias, and worse—laughing at its ambition. Modern academic scholarship frowns upon the scope and conjecture of Roscher, and it especially disapproves of the comparative study of motifs, which is a basic tenet of depth psychology and a basic method employed by all psychoanalytic investigations from Roheim through Neumann. The academics insist upon their departments: a myth or motif or figure shall be studied within its historical, cultural, textual, linguistic, economic, formal, sociological, or what-have-you context, but anathema it is to compare the mythical motif or figure with those of another period, area or culture or to regard a myth, motif, or figure as relevant primarily for the human psyche and its imagination.

For depth psychology, however, the themes and personages of mythology are not mere subjects of knowledge. They are living actualities of the human being, having existence as psychic realities in addition to and perhaps even prior to their historical and geographical manifestation. Depth psychology turns to mythology less to learn about others in the past than to understand ourselves in the present. Roscher's investigation of ancient Pan in connection with the contemporary nightmare is just a case in point.

The academic treatment of myth in terms of departments of knowledge results in a plethora of theories of myth and in various explanatory fallacies. We have each been treated to many of these. It is hardly possible to find a myth recounted today without having to suffer within the same breath as its telling an interpretation of its meaning. Paramount among the various fallacies is simplification.

The complexity of a mytheme, or of a personage in it, is presented as an account of a social, economic, or historical process, or a pre-rational witness to some philosophical contention or moralistic instruction. Myths are assumed to be disguised expositions of natural science, metaphysics, tribal superbia, gender oppression, or religion. But before each of these applications of mythical meaning, there is the myth itself and its naked effect within soul, which, in the first place, created the myth, and in the second place, perpetuated it with embellishments; and soul still re-dreams these themes in its fantasy, behavior, and thought structures.

The primary approach to myth thus must be psychological, since the psyche provides both its original source and its continually living context. Here, however, a psychological approach does not mean a simplified exchange of terms, exotic metaphors cashed in for the common currency of familiar concepts, the big made small for easy application.

A psychological approach, as I understand it, does not mean a psychological interpretation. It does not mean to take myth over into the department of psychology or into a school of depth analysis, preparing a new series of psychological reductions equal in their narrowness to the other departmental simplifications (couched in technical conceits) that I would challenge. As myth belongs more to *theoria* than to pragmatics, so its understanding belongs more to exegesis and hermeneutics than to formulaic interpretation.

A psychological approach means what it says: a way through the psyche into myth, a connection with myth that proceeds via soul, including especially its bizarre fantasy and its suffering (psychopathology), an unwrapping and leading out of the soul into mythical significance and vice versa. Only when the psyche realizes itself as enacting mythemes can it understand myth, so that a psychological exegesis of myth begins with the exegesis of oneself, soul-making. And, from the other side: only when myth is led back into soul, only when myth has psychological significance does it become a living reality, necessary for life, rather than a literary, philosophical, or religious artifice. Scholarship belongs within this process as part of the psychological approach. How else approximate mythical reality than by immersion in its field, the contexts which breed it, the imagery it has shown throughout history. Scholarship then becomes a method of soul-making rather than mainly a method of knowing. The therapeutic revivification of the psyche and the renascence of myth—two inseparable processes that may be one and the same for insighting what we know are as important as knowing.

The value of scholarship is thus to be judged not only for its contribution to intellect but as well for its contribution to imagination. This should be borne in mind when reading Roscher. Ideally the two kinds of contribution should add to each other, but often modern Classical scholars see the exorbitant fantasies of their forbears in the field as intellectual faults. They do not see that the reverse is taking place in themselves: the poverty of fantasy, the psychological simplicities, the very dryness of their touch in the midst of their intellectual accomplishments expose imaginal faults no less serious. When this is the case, we readers should not turn away from scholarly books but instead learn how to read them. We can read them as part of the psychological approach, both experiencing the effect on imagination of the intellectual data and noting the imaginative fantasy within which the author organizes and by which data is implicitly interpreted. No matter who deals with myth and no matter how unimaginative the approach, the imaginal world is struck, and it echoes in what is being said. We cannot touch myth without it touching us.

Though we may query the speculative nature of nineteenth-century scholarship and take it to task for an adventurousness that the sophisticated, skeptical—and maybe cynical—mind obtaining in the field today would hardly dare, we should not forget that the late nineteenth-century psychiatrists, archaeologists, ethnologists, and mythologists were carried by tremendous passion. They were not mere academic workers. Nor was their drive mere obsession with knowledge, and through knowledge, authority, and from there to eminence and power. There seems to have been something else breaking into our age through them, some vision, some essential question about the depths of human nature.

Or, was theirs a search for lost gods? Perhaps the fascination with the unknown depths indicated something further than the secular humanism of their intentions, reaching into impersonal, inhuman dimensions of soul where heathen, pagan, and mythic figures still moved and still drew their devotees, even if in the academic garb of impartial scholarship. Psychology may not take the reports of scholars at their literal face value only; we regard their passion for discovery as archetypally governed. Like the alchemists, the explorers and the crusaders in earlier centuries who also took their activities and goals literally, the investigators of the nineteenth-century were engaged not only in "scientific research" but as well in a psychological quest into a new terrain of "depth."

These depths were projected, as we now would say, into the remote past, into mythology, into foreign dark tribes and exotic customs, into the simple folk and their lore, and into the mentally alienated. The thorough exploration of any of these fields of scholarship is also a thorough exploration of human personality in its obscure reaches, where it merges with the impersonal background of life at its "primitive" level in the childhood of thought and language, of persons and society. Roscher's thoroughness, as Frazer's, or James Cook's, or Emil Kraepelin's in psychiatry, may better be seen as a driven attempt to encompass human depths, to chart what has been called the unconscious. Like Arthur Evans in Crete or Heinrich Schliemann at Troy, they were driven by the private fantasies of imagination to rediscover an imaginal world. Even if performing in a scientific, sober, and scholarly manner, these towering professorial figures of the late nineteenth century with their massive written output, their systematizations, and their hunger for work reincorporated into Western consciousness that which had been excluded since the Renaissance: the imaginal and its power in life. Their research led to the recognition that humanity was not only Western, modern, secular, civilized, and sane but also primitive, archaic, mythical, magical, and mad. Paradoxically they used the most advanced methods of reason to establish the reality of the irrational – or that which had to be called the irrational because of the shrunken definition of reason determined by that century's positivism, mechanism, and utilitarianism.

If the psychiatry of the period did not produce new cures for insanity despite (or because of) its classificatory zeal, neither did the history of religion, linguistics, anthropology, and Classical studies reawaken the dying rituals and beliefs of other cultures or transform these aspects of ours. But a cure, a re-awakening, did come about as a reconstruction of Western consciousness, which, because of the rediscovery of the imaginal function of soul, could no longer identify itself with its former one-sided psychic structure. The mind with an ego at its center had lost its moorings; things were splitting up, and psychiatry discovered schizophrenia as that century came to its close. A new relativism was at hand: there were other myths than the Bible, other gods than Christ, other peoples than white, and, within each individual, there were other kinds of consciousness with diverse intentions and values.

Roscher, it would seem, did not intend his work to hasten this process of disintegration. Quite the opposite. He complained in his 1908 preface to Volume 3.1 of the *Lexikon* of the "unpropitiousness of the present" for work such as his. He saw around him "an ever-increasing turning away from what hitherto had been the foundation of our higher education and culture, i.e., Classical antiquity, the Renaissance, and the indigenous classics of literature and art." These constituted for him the bulwark against the "abyss of barbarism." But he did not see that, though his method was reasoned and ordered, his material was Olympus itself, nay, the entire corpus of ancient polytheism whose resurrection was his life's work. For more than two thousand years Judeo-Christianity had bent its will toward the repression of this pagan past which now thanks to Roscher was conveniently packaged in a *Lexikon*. It seems as if his intellect had no notion of the possible effects upon the imagination. Like a detached natural scientist operating upon the primordial elements of fissionable materials, Roscher had painstakingly assembled (and made available to everyone who could subscribe) the stuff for psychic detonations no less dynamic for the fate of culture. Roscher's early association with Nietzsche is thus no accident; they founded more than a Philology Club.

Yet Roscher's use of mythology for the defense of culture is still valid, even if not in quite the way he intended. We return to mythical roots not merely for knowledge of the classics but for the psychological reality that is their context. In this reality myth is paramount, and the polytheistic imagination, which he systematically catalogued, plays a role equal with reason and feeling. The defense of culture then lies less in tightening the rational order, less in extending the rule of human feeling, than it does in exploring and charting the imaginal. We must know the archetypal substructures that govern our reactions; we must recognize the gods and the myths in which we are embroiled. Without this awareness, our behavior becomes wholly mythic and consciousness a delusion. When Christ was the operative myth, it was enough to know his modes and those of the Devil. We had the Christian structure for our reflection. But now that this single model of consciousness has dissociated into the root multiples that lay dormant below it and are presented by mythology, we cannot get by without mythological reflection upon our patterns of reaction, our attitudes, our fantasies.

Although Roscher was a contemporary of Freud (born eleven years later in 1856), Roscher's work, like that of the other pioneers, differs in one significant way from the great psychologists, Freud and Jung, who too belong in this scholarly line by virtue of their prodigious output, scholarly method, speculative daring – and concern with culture. Freud and Jung knew they were writing about themselves even when discussing Moses and Job. Could Roscher have conceived Pan or any of the antique figures he elaborated to be "his problem" in the same way? This kind of psychological identification—and distance—was possible not even for Nietzsche, while the other contemporaries in anthropology, history of religion, psychopathology, and mythology still enjoyed the Cartesian delusion that their work and their psychology could be held separale. They were still carried by the fantasy of subject and object. Scholarship, like natural science, retains a vested psychological interest in the "objective fantasy," by means of which investigators can still defend themselves against learning through their research something about themselves and not only about their material.

Unfortunately, the pioneers combined the childhood of thought and language, of individuals and society too literally. They believed that actual childhood of humanity (Freud), of language (Max Müller), or of culture in "primitives," antiquity, or in archaeology would reveal the key. They were still laboring under an "origins of the species" fantasy, and they too easily interchanged at a literal level the child, the primitive, the mythical, and the insane. This interchange has caused immeasurable confusion about so-called "primitive" thinking, about childhood, about mental aberration, and also about myth. They did not enough realize that their scholarly activities were also psychological, and that the origins and the childhood they were seeking to elaborate were also psychological, i.e., "child" and "origin" and "primitive" as psychic factors that are prior to, and perhaps *a priori* within, the rational intellect performing the inquiry. They assumed they were studying subjects "out there" in archaeological digs, asylum patients, Classical texts, whereas they were at the same time studying the subject "in here," in search of the primordial child of the imaginal level, of the psyche whose mythical mode of perception provides the archetypal origins within science itself. So these researchers at the pinnacle of their scientific scholarship were preparing its collapse. For the imaginal forces which their inquiries led to (whether in anthropology, psychiatry, or Classical religion) eventually threw into question the rational, adult and civilized man of the Enlightenment, his method and even his mind. Roscher's work on *Ephialtes* is a piece of the process that undermined the nineteenth century and opened the way for the irrationality of the twentieth.

Preface

A detailed preoccupation for many years with the myth and cult of Pan—the old Greek god of herds and herdsmen—has led other investigators and myself to an enquiry into his function as Ephialtes, the demon or evil spirit of nightmares. To attain a basic understanding of this function, it now seems absolutely imperative to master as thoroughly as possible the field of the Greek and Roman presentations of nightmares and demons; I have, therefore, sought to assemble all that antiquity has preserved for us concerning Ephialtes and to form this into a clear picture, which I now offer to the public. I was obliged to do this because Ludwig Laistner, the learned and ingenious author of *The Riddle of the Sphinx,* did not succeed, despite his valiant efforts, in dealing with and clarifying the Greek and Roman traditions and conceptions about nightmares and demons in sufficiently strict a manner for scholarly requirements. This deficiency, in a work meritorious in many respects, is due to two reasons: first, because of his understandable and excusable position as a specialist in Germanic studies, Laistner was able to draw only from the sphere of German mythology as a whole, inasmuch as he lacked an obvious and fundamental knowledge of the Greek and Roman sources; and secondly, because he attempted to write a work that would appeal to a very large number of people. Closely connected with this is the fact that Laistner's style is more literary than scholarly. His writing is always stimulating, but frequently the desirable moderation and strict self-criticism of a genuinely scholarly work is lacking. This is true not merely of his Greek and Latin words and proper names—at times much too daring and sometimes full of unsupported etymology but also of his total failure to elevate the dream, and in particular the nightmare, to the main and fundamental principle of all mythology. For these reasons I was compelled to disregard and avoid Laistner's book in my treatment of nightmares and demons; and I had rather to limit myself and only occasionally borrow individual and valuable German and Slavic parallels. Here and there I have been obliged to mention the views and explanations of Laistner and either to agree with or to dissociate myself from them.

My research falls under four main chapters. In the first I have tried to unravel the essence, origin, and constituent elements of the nightmare on the basis of observations made by more recent medical practitioners; in the second chapter, on the other hand, my objective has been to furnish proof that the views of the ancient physicians—which are all more or less dependent on Soranus—are to a great extent in harmony with the modern ones. This chapter has also an instructive collection and precise analysis of the nightmares of antiquity handed down in literature, for the critical examination of their extremely diverse fund of ideas. Among these is the nightmare related of Jacob (Genesis 32: 23ff.) wrestling with Elohim. The third chapter interprets etymologically the Greek and Roman designations of nightmares and demons, such as Ephialtes, (H)pialos, Epheles, Tiphus, Pnigalion, Baphugnas, Inuus, Incubo, Faunus ficarius, and others. These are subjected to a thorough examination and are explained etymologically on the basis of present views on the essence of the nightmare. The fourth chapter deals in detail with those demons of the Greeks and Romans to whom in the first place the excitation of nightmares was ascribed (Pan, Satyr, Faunus, Silvanus) and aims to answer why especially these demons have become the demons of the nightmare.

1

The Nature and Origin of the Nightmare from the Modern Medical Aspect

In the past I have often used the applied method in discussions of mythological and religious-historical themes; this method was to proceed from the basic and objective consideration of the inner and outer experiences and facts that lie at the basis of an enquiry into mythic and religious conceptions. In the same frame of mind I now wish first of all to try and explain as objectively as possible the observations and experiences of modern and ancient medicine in relation to the origin and nature of the nightmare. I have placed the modern views at the start of this investigation, not simply because they are derived from a wide and comprehensive actual observation of facts, but because they are also less suspect of uncritical, untenable, and obsolete theories of biased observation than are those of the ancient physicians. At the same time we will achieve in this way a rather more accurate yardstick for the critical examination of the theories established by the physicians of the classical era in relation to these aspects of the nightmare.

For the most essential particulars concerning the nature and origin of the nightmare we are indebted primarily to Johann Börner,[1] who in 1855 in his inaugural dissertation enunciated the essential points that, as far as I am aware, are accepted by all the authorities on medical and psychological science. Börner obtained his main results partly through personal observation, having himself frequently suffered from severe forms of nightmare, and partly from observing fellow sufferers in the throes of a nightmare. By these means and after the most critical study of the conditions under which a nightmare arises, he was finally able to bring about nightmares whenever he so desired, that is to say, experimentally. On the basis of numerous observations made on himself and on other people, Börner described the character of the nightmare as follows:

The onset may be at any time during the night and usually commences with the feeling of troublesome breathing...It is generally thought that the attack starts when lying on one's back, whereas in reality lying face downwards is the more frequent position. The increase of dyspnea secondarily rouses the imagination—the dream—which motivates a large variety of reasons for the dyspnea. The most common (but by no means exclusive) dream is that in which the person sees some hairy animal. This is often a dog who in an inconceivable manner has arrived in the room and slowly and deliberately creeps up upon the bed to sit on the person's chest, usually on the area of the jugular vein. This is then taken to be the cause of the difficulty in breathing and the pressure (*Alpdruck*) that has become proverbial. Frequently there is a vision of some disgusting creature, an ugly human being, an old woman, or just a simple burden setting itself down on the chest...Anxiety increases with the degree of dyspnea, and sweating, palpitation, turgescence of the face and swelling of the nerves at the neck set in. The victim feels a need to alter his position so that he can shake off the oppressive agent and he is firmly convinced that this will bring relief. The muscles concerned, however, refuse to react to the most strenuous efforts of the will. This likewise contributes to the unrelieved anxiety...Finally the extreme anxiety and the accompanying interrupted sleep bring about a violent movement produced with great effort and preceded by plaintive moans, which usually results in an immediate and extremely pleasant feeling of relief and ease and is followed either by waking up or by continued sleep. When both sleep and dream are uninterrupted, it is frequently most difficult to convince oneself that the visions seen were not real.[2]

According to other observers, the feeling of deliverance is ushered in by a loud cry.[3] Macnish in his book on dreams says:

At the moment of throwing off the fit, we seem to turn round upon our sides with a mighty effort, as if from beneath the pressure of a superincumbent weight; and the more thoroughly to awake ourselves, we generally kick violently, beat our breasts, rise up in the bed, and cry out once or twice. As soon as we are able to exercise our volitions or voice with freedom, the paroxysm is at an end.[4]

As regards the origin of nightmares in otherwise healthy people, Börner arrived at the conclusion from precise observation of himself "that since the trouble always disappeared suddenly after a vigorous movement, it follows that a hindrance to respiration must have been removed."[5] Further, observation of himself showed "that during a nightmare, the external orifices of respiration—the nose and mouth—were more or less completely covered. When I was lying on my back or on my side, this was caused by the bedclothes pressing quite firmly over my face, or more frequently by lying face downwards with my face pushed into the pillow."[6] Dealing with this point, Macnish says:

> I have frequently had attacks of this disorder while sitting in an armchair or with my head leaning against a table. In fact, these are the most likely positions to bring it on, the lungs being then more completely compressed than in almost any other posture. I have also had it most distinctly while lying on the side, and I know many cases of a similar description in others.[7]

Börner, on the other hand, asserts that, according to his observations, lying face downwards is the most frequent position for the nightmare. Börner's studies on himself were completely confirmed by successful experiments on other people and were cleared of the suspicion of subjectivity and self-deception. By covering the mouth and nose of other people, Börner in many instances succeeded in producing exactly the same signs that he had observed on himself. In these cases the nightmare was a peculiar bastard animal—half dog and half monkey—that did not, as before, slowly slink up to the bed, but sprang in one leap upon the breast of the victim without being previously noticed (as the result of covering the patient's face). This sudden leaping jump of the nightmare is characteristic of the majority of cases and hence the Greek word "Ephialtes"—"the one who jumps up"—is very apt. The animal then remained quiet as if sleeping on his victim while the unfortunate person, out of sheer anxiety, did not dare to move until finally the animal fell down as the result of some movement executed at the height of the torture.

The form attributed by the dreamer to the nightmare depended mainly upon the articles Börner used to cover the face.

> Cloth of a coarse or shaggy quality always brought on the apparition of an animal with hair, such as a poodle or cat. If the mouth and nose were covered by the hand alone, this dream picture of a hairy animal did not arise, but was generally replaced by that of another human being who was ugly and hostile and who seized and throttled the sleeper. When only a small area of the respiratory orifices was gradually covered, there arose a mild degree of anxiety and dyspnea with a corresponding incapability of movement...In this case

the phantom generally entered the room slowly and at ease. It then looked around for some time until it finally occurred to it to haunt the person lying on the bed. But if the covering of the mouth and nose is such that it causes marked dyspnea, the phantom is instantly in the room and upon the sleeper's chest; thus the dreamer cannot give any information as to how the phantom arrived there. These apparitions are very vivid, but their course is short.[8]

Occasionally—and more commonly in women—the feeling of anxiety is coupled with that of lust, and women often believe that the phantom has had sexual intercourse with them. Men have analogous sensations and generally emissions of semen resulting from the pressure exerted on the genitalia by lying on the abdomen.[9]

Börner states that the main symptoms of the nightmare are the feeling of pressure generally brought about by lying face downward, inability to move, and anxiety. Macnish calls particular attention to the extraordinary and inexplicable anxiety of the patient as a symptom that is practically never absent.[10] An essential prerequisite for the origin of a nightmare is deep sleep.

The experiences and observations of other doctors and psychologists have supplemented and confirmed Börner's studies, which were carried out only on clinically normal people. It is almost generally admitted that the difficulty in breathing, which produces a nightmare in healthy people and is caused by an external impediment like bedclothes, can also originate from certain illnesses and likewise give rise to very severe nightmares. Examples of these illnesses are croup, tuberculosis, organic heart disease, asthmatic complaints, advanced stages of hypochondria and hysteria, mental illnesses, and fever deliria. Börner adds: "Thus I believe that there will be a kind of nightmare preceding suffocation by gases, just like the sudden nocturnal shutting off of the respiratory tracts by foreign bodies, croupous membranes, etc."[11] According to Binz, one can see in the deliria of typhoid fever the same symptoms as in poisoning by the thorn-apple, i.e., confused sensual dreams, intoxication, and narcotization.[12] Occasionally a nightmare can result from a faulty diet, as for example from the intake of indigestible food.

Binz indeed asserts on the basis of his experiences that when he is suffering from a head-cold, a rather heavy evening meal is sufficient to produce a nightmare. He says:

The state of dreaming we know under the term of nightmare can be produced by acute poisoning...The validity of Börner's researches can be established by paying some attention to oneself. If, when one is suffering from a cold that obstructs both nasal openings, one eats a rather heavy evening meal and then goes to sleep while the nose is reasonably free from obstruction and the mouth closed as usual, it will frequently happen that catarrhal secretion and swelling of the nasal mucous membrane occurs during the deepest sleep. The passage of the air becomes more and more obstructed and the carbon dioxide and other suffocating products of metabolism accumulate in the blood and insult the nervous system. A profound uneasiness pervades our mind in completely blurred forms; sometimes this takes the form of a definite process of suffocation, at other times the uneasiness remains obscure and confused in accordance with the duration and strength of its origin. Eventually a sudden movement of the body is imparted to the closed lips, or more often—as I have observed repeatedly on myself—there is a loud cry of fear and need of assistance which opens the mouth to allow the rescuing atmospheric air a free pathway. Oxygen is the antidote. The oxygen equalizes the perverted irritation caused by excretions retained in the cells of our brain; it does this by binding with and chemically altering the excretions.[13]

As we shall see later, this theory was already formulated by the physicians of ancient times.

A special feature to which attention has been called by most observers is the unusually vivid nature of nightmare visions that frequently far surpass the impressions left by what is experienced while awake. Laistner says in this connection:

The intensity of the apparitions in nightmares is far greater than in the ordinary dream images, so much so that the subject when awake is fully convinced that he has not simply had a dream. The impression exceeds the most vivid intuition of the person's waking imagination, however extraordinarily "mythic" that may be, and so there can be no doubt that the living belief in nightmare monsters can be explained most simply by the vividness of the dream presentations.[14]

Thus Macnish recounts an actual observation by the physician Waller, who had a nightmare apparition, which he mistook for reality for a long time until he finally realized that it was only a dream. Macnish also states:

> Sometimes we are in a state closely approximating perfect sleep; at other times we are almost completely awake; and it will be observed that the more awake we are, the greater is the violence of the paroxysm. I have frequently experienced the affection stealing upon me while in perfect possession of my faculties and have undergone the greatest torture.[15]

This view of Macnish seems to some extent to be endorsed by Cubasch, who says in *Der Alp* (The Nightmare):

> Dream pictures often seem to continue after awakening; this is a peculiarity that is not only associated with nightmares, but is often observed in vivid dreams of all kinds. This continuation of the visions must be attributed to sleep-drunkenness, which is the state between being fully awake and deeply asleep or the reverse. It demonstrates only that a person has not yet ceased to dream and that sleep has not yet been completely shaken off. The conditions most favorable for this state are provided when a person is suddenly aroused from deep sleep either by alarming dreams or by other circumstances.[16]

The so-called pavores nocturni (night terrors) of children between the ages of three and seven years seem to belong in this context. Of these Soltmann says:

> They usually occur during the deepest sleep and several hours after falling asleep, without any prior warning. The children commonly sit up suddenly in bed about midnight with a flushed face and bathed in sweat. Their fixed gaze, the confused talk, the absence of response to calls and questions, all indicate that consciousness is dulled. The carotid blood vessels pulsate, the heart beats strongly, and the hands tremble with terror. Persuasion is of no avail and the senses remain spellbound under the heavy pressure of terror and fright brought about by the vision. Sometimes the children will utter monosyllabic garbled sounds and words—like "there, there," "dog," "man," etc.—which obviously relate to the alarming visions. It often requires fifteen to twenty minutes to calm down the child.[17]

Soltmann further points out that the majority of these children suffer from indigestion, dyspepsia, constipation, gastritis, anaemia, scrofula, and rickets. Occasionally these night terrors occur in typhoid fever, scarlet fever, and in psychic excitement produced by fright and fear. A twelve-year-old boy afflicted with advanced spondylitis dorsalis imagined during his attacks that an animal had jumped on his back and wanted to crush him to death. It can be seen from this how closely related children's night terrors are to the nightmare. Compare Tylor: "Some say these 'mury' come by night to men, sit upon their breasts and suck their blood, while others think it is only children's blood they suck, they being to grown people mere nightmares."[18] The sucking of children's blood, as Tylor points out, relates to certain emaciating diseases of childhood. To return to the main subject of our theme—

> ...dream pictures play with the half-awake consciousness, and the mind is made to believe things that do not exist in reality. Thus the forms or shapes of that fanciful world of fairy stories in which a person saw himself transfigured remain as an echo before his clouded consciousness, and the person thinks he is observing these things fully awake, whereas in fact he is not yet quite fully conscious. Sleep-drunkenness is a fruitful soil for all kinds of deceptions of the senses ...A person in the state of sleep-drunkenness who is fully convinced that he is master of himself is seeing just the phantoms that assailed him while he was asleep; and he sees them now with his eyes open and with apparently normal consciousness.[19]

In his *Physiologie der Nervenfasern* (Physiology of Nerve Fibers), H. Meyer[20] gives many characteristic examples of this continuation of the dream apparition after awaking. I need scarcely call special attention to the fact that, after waking, such phenomena remain for some time and are directly on the borderline between a dream and a hallucination—that is to say, between normal consciousness and disturbed consciousness. They differ merely quantitatively from the hallucinations of insanity by their shorter duration; if they continue to persist undiminished over a period of days, weeks or months, they must be looked upon as an undoubted sign of insanity. At this point it is well to heed the fact that "frequently dreams are blamed by mental patients as the starting points of certain fixed ideas, in so far as what is dreamt is thought to have been a genuine experience."[21]

As regards the dangers of nightmares when these occur frequently and are very intense, Börner[22] thinks that a severe degree of dyspnea with its attendant retarding of the blood circulation could easily give rise to cerebral hemorrhage and possibly even acute edema of the brain.

According to Radestock,[23] nightmares sometimes precede mental illness and occur in organic cardiac diseases, asthmatic syndromes, and repeatedly in the more advanced stages of hypochondria and hysteria. Macnish[24] is of the opinion that they can produce apoplexy or may be the cause of epileptic and hysteric attacks in people who are unusually sensitive.

Finally, may I add a few words about what has been observed more recently concerning the composition of the nightmare apparition. This, as described by Macnish,[25] who himself suffered greatly from nightmares, is extraordinarily variegated but in general two types of nightmares can be differentiated: one dreadful and highly alarming, the other milder, more benevolent, and at times even voluptuous (erotic). The nightmare creates a frightful and alarming impression especially when a hairy animal appears in it, such as a black shaggy dog (poodle)— the most usual form of embodiment for evil demons. Other frequent forms are the cat, marten, hedgehog, mouse, bear, he-goat, pig, horse, tiger, snake, toad, eel, dragon, or finally a peculiar hybrid that is half dog, half monkey. The shape or form of the animal in which the nightmare incarnates itself, seems—as we have already seen—to depend essentially on the nature of the respiratory obstruction that produces the dyspnea, as for example, the quality of the bedclothes impeding the mouth and nose. These may be either smooth and soft or coarse and hard. Meyer[26] explains that the apparition of a hedgehog can easily arise if the dreamer is lying face downwards on prickly straw. The opposite is the nightmare demon clothed in mole fur, which naturally corresponds to an obstruction to breathing by a very smooth material. When occasionally the apparition shows itself in the form of an inanimate object—such as a wisp of straw, a down feather, or smoke—this can easily be explained by the sleeper waking up from the nightmare and holding in his clenched fingers a piece of straw or a feather that has come from his bedding. He will imagine such objects to be the final form assumed by the nightmare demon which he has grasped, or he imagines that the smoke filling the bedroom and tormenting him on awakening by hindering his breathing is the last metamorphosis of the demon.

If the specter appears in human shape, it can assume forms that are extraordinarily diverse. Sometimes it is a man and sometimes a woman; it can be ugly or beautiful; at times it is a dwarflike goblin of scarcely human form, or it may be an enormous giant. The apparition may be dumb or it may enter into conversation with the dreamer. Börner says in this connection that "only in rare instances is the monster barbaric and the woman sometimes even lovable. In such cases the monster talks and is occasionally so incautious as to unveil the future to the haunted person. Here the apparition is looked upon as an emissary of the god-head from whom torments as well as benefits are accepted with a willing heart."[27] The form may be that of a living being or of a dead one. This has naturally led to the supposition that the living—for example, witches—as well as the dead possess the power of appearing to a sleeper in a dream and tormenting him. Thus Spitta reports that an eighteen-year-old girl in an advanced stage of tuberculosis and having great difficulty in breathing experienced, whenever she fell asleep, the horrible dream of her dead grandmother coming in through the window and kneeling on her chest in order to crush her to death.[28] Another nightmare given by Radestock was the following:

> Once in the early hours of the morning I saw appear before me at the foot of my bed a hideous small brute of barely human form. It seemed to me to be of medium height and to have a thin neck, spare figure, very dark eyes, and a narrow, wrinkled brow. The nose was broad, the mouth large, the lips pouting, and the chin short and pointed. Furthermore it had a goatbeard, upright pointed ears—like Pan—dirty dry hair, dog's teeth, a pointed occiput, a projected chest, a humped back, withered hips, and wore dirty clothing. The phantom took hold of the edge of my bed, shook the bed with tremendous force and said: "You will not remain here much longer!"As soon as I awoke from terror...I sprang out of the bed, hurried to the cloister and threw myself down before the altar and remained there a long time, numbed by fear.[29]

Collective apparitions are sometimes met with in the nightmare, just as in what has been called the panicky terrors and mental disorders. This means that a large number of people are attacked at the same time by the nightmare—just as in an epidemic—and that these people all have the same visions. On the basis of such "collective apparitions," A. Krauss[30] assumes that a specific *Alpmiasma* (nightmare miasma) gives rise to these apparitions. An interesting example of the condition is seen in the following report by Radestock:

A complete battalion of French soldiers quartered in an old abbey near Tropea in Calabria was attacked by a nightmare during the middle hours of the night. The whole battalion to a man arose from their beds and, chased by panicky terror, ran out into the open. (Note here the close link between the nightmare and the panicky terror of man and animals.) When questioned what had so frightened them, they replied one and all that the devil in the shape of a large black shaggy dog had entered through the door, rushed on their chests with the speed of lightning and then disappeared through a door opposite the entrance. The same scene was repeated on the following night. Notwithstanding the fact that the officers had distributed themselves on all sides to stand watch against the devil, no power on earth could make the soldiers return to their quarters. This extraordinary manifestation is explained very simply. These soldiers had, on a hot June day, done a forced march of 25 miles and were then crowded into the abbey, which was too small for so large a number. They had lain down to sleep on a little straw and had not taken off their clothes because they had nothing with which to cover themselves. The exhaustion, the primitive sleeping conditions, and the constricting uniforms all caused physiological excitation, which soon produced an apparition already known to the troops, since the locals had told them that they would experience something uncanny in the abbey where the devil prowled in the guise of a black shaggy dog.[31]

The erotic dreams described by Börner as occasionally associated with nightmares can be divided into two types according to the sex of the erotic demon who appears. This depends generally—but not necessarily—upon the sex of the sleeper. Hence even today Germanic superstition differentiates between the female (*mare*) and the male (*mar*) love phantom. The former is by far the more frequent. According to a medieval and current popular belief, devils and witches— i.e., daemonic living beings—appear in both forms to seduce or torment the sleeper in his or her dream. (The *incubus* and *succuba* of the Middle Ages come to mind.) Indeed, there exist numerous partly highly romantic fairytales and legends in which the sleepers fall in love with the love-phantom and even have offspring by it. Obviously some of these are often the result of organic sexual complaints, as Krauss in particular demonstrates in his "Der Sinn im Wahnsinn."[32] As examples I quote here only two well-established instances, one of which was observed by no less an authority than Jean-Étienne Dominique Esquirol. In the first of these, a mentally affected woman with uterine disease asserted in all seriousness that she had been the Devil's wife for a million years, had slept with him every night, and had born him fifteen children. The other case comes from Radestock, who describes how Salomon Maimonides, having been occupied with the Kabbalah over a long period, dreamed that the devil Lilith fell upon him, while at another time after being engaged in exalted ideas he enjoyed in a dream the gracious embrace of the angelic Shekinah.[33] There is a specially noteworthy example of a sensual dream mixed with erotic feelings (physical intercourse with Christ) also to be found in Radestock.[34] Comparison may also be made with the fables around the births of Merlin and Robert the Devil.

1. J. Börner, *Über das Alpdrücken, seine Begründung und Verhütung* (Würzburg: Carl Joseph Becker, 1885).

2. Ibid., 895.

3. C. Binz, *Ueber den Traum* (Bonn: Adolph Marcus, 1878), 26f.

4. R. Macnish, *The Philosophy of Sleep* (Glasgow: W.R. M'Phun, 1845), 130.

5. Börner, *Über das Alpdrücken*, 15ff.

6. Ibid., 17.

7. Macnish, *The Philosophy of Sleep*, 131–32.

8. Börner, *Über das Alpdrücken*, 22.

9. Ibid., 12.

10. Macnish, *The Philosophy of Sleep*, 125.

11. Börner, *Über das Alpdrücken*, 28.

12. Binz, *Ueber den Traum*, 17.

13. Ibid., 26ff.

14. L. Laistner, *Das Rätsel der Sphinx: Grundzüge einer Mythengeschichte* (Berlin: Verlag von Wilhelm Hertz, 1889), 1: x.

15. Macnish, *The Philosophy of Sleep*, 136.

16. C. Cubasch, *Der Alp* (Berlin: Habel, 1877), 25.

17. See the article on "Night Terrors" by Soltmann, in *Real-Encyclopädie der gesammten Heilkunde*, ed. A. Eulenburg (Vienna and Leipzig: Urban & Schwarzenberg, 1880), 14: 425.

18. E.B. Tylor, *Primitive Culture: Researches into the Development of Mythology, Philosophy, Religion, Language, Art, and Culture* (London: John Murray, 1903), 2:192.

19. Cubasch, *Der Alp*, 25.

20. G.H. Meyer, *Untersuchungen über die Physiologie der Nervenfaser* (Tübingen: Verlag der Laupp'schen Buchhandlung, 1843), 309.

21. See the article on "Delirium" by Mendel, in *Real-Encyclopädie der gesammten Heilkunde,* 5:464.

22. Börner, *Über das Alpdrücken,* 10.

23. Paul Radestock, *Schlaf und Traum: Eine physiologisch-psychologische Untersuchung* (Leipzig: Breitkopf und Härtel, 1879), 130.

24. Macnish, *The Philosophy of Sleep,* 142.

25. Ibid., 125.

26. E. H. Meyer, *Germanische Mythologie* (Berlin: Mayer und Müller, 1891), par. 107.

27. Börner, *Über das Alpdrücken,* 11.

28. H. Spitta, *Die Schlaf- und Traumzustände der menschlichen Seele: Mit besonderer Berücksichtigung ihres Verhältnisses zu den psychischen Alienationen* (Tübingen: Franz Fues, 1882), 242.

29. Radestock, *Schlaf und Traum,* 126.

30. A. Krauss, "Der Sinn in Wahnsinn: Eine psychiatrische Untersuchung," *Allgemeine Zeitschrift für Psychiatrie* 15 (1858): 632.

31. Radestock, *Schlaf und Traum,* 126.

32. A. Krauss, "Der Sinn in Wahnsinn," 618.

33. Radestock, *Schlaf und Traum,* 128.

34. Ibid., 289 n133.

2

*The Nature and Origin of the Nightmare
According to the Ancient Physicians*

Having objectively established the current theories on the nature and origin of the nightmare, we are now in a firm position to criticize the attitude of the ancient physicians.

The first Greek physician who we know for certain to have dealt with the nightmare in his scientific research was Themison of Laodicea. He was the founder of the so-called Methodical School and a contemporary of Caesar and Cicero. Unfortunately, all we know is that in his letters he called the nightmare not *ephialtes* ("leaper"), as did other doctors, but employed a rarer but, at the same time, rather characteristic term: *pnigalion* ("throttler"). We obtain much more exact information from the theories of the leading member of the school, Soranus, who, next to Hippocrates and Galen, was perhaps the most productive and significant of the ancient physicians. His views, long known to us from the Latin adaptation of Caelius Aurelianus (5th century)[35] and to a great extent from later medical text books, especially from the works of Paulus Aegineta (7th century), Oreibasius (4th century) and of Aetius (beginning of the 6th century).

In the era before Soranus, incidentally, Rufus of Ephesus had also considered the nightmare. Compare the extant fragment of Rufus from the excerpts of the Arab Rhazes, which Darmberg and Ruelle quote in their edition of Rufus: "When someone is plagued by the incubus, prescribe emetics and laxatives, put the patient on a light diet, purge the head by sneezing and gargling, and later rub in beaver oil and the like to prevent epilepsy."

We have also an account of the nightmare in the late Byzantine monk and philosopher, Mikhael Psellos (11th century), and in the second installment of the *Anecdota Graeca et Graecolatina*, vol. II (Berlin, 1870), edited by Valentin Rose, in which we find various reminiscences of the nightmare theory of Soranos.

Concerning the views of the ancients on the nature of the nightmare, the very expression *pnigalion*, which Themison probably borrowed from the vernacular, shows that he considered "choking, becoming strangled" as the most essential characteristic of the nightmare, the symptom to which Soranus, Oreibasius, Aetius, Paulus Aegineta, and others have also drawn special attention. Further symptoms mentioned are the feelings of the sleeper that somebody is sitting on his chest or suddenly jumps upon it or that somebody climbs up and crushes him heavily with his weight. The sufferer feels incapacity to move, torpidity, and inability to speak. Attempts to speak often result only in single, inarticulate sounds. According to Soranus and Paulus Aegineta, the impression may arise that the demon sitting on the sleeper's chest is trying to violate him but vanishes as soon as the sleeper seizes his fingers or joins his own hands or clenches his fists: "Some are so affected by empty visions that they believe they are being attacked and forced to the vilest acts: if they grasp the oppressor they believe it will vanish."[36] The passage is absolutely clear and obviously means that according to popular belief the person tortured by the nightmare must grasp the monster with his fingers if he is to chase it away. This belief is also current in Germany and among the Slavs. Laistner says: "He whom the Murawa oppresses must touch her small toe, and then she leaves him." "One must hold firmly the finger of Psezpolnica (a Slavonic female spirit) and then she flees." "One must seize the Murawa or nightmare witch or hold her fast by the hair."[37] The expression "with closed fingers," quoted from Paulus Aegineta, is not so easy to explain because it is not clear whether he refers to the fingers of the nightmare demon or to those of the victim. If the former, it is virtually identical with the words of Soranus; if the latter, we are reminded of the ancient superstition that folding the hands or clenching the fists was an effective antidote for magic. According to Wuttke,[38] the nightmare can be dispelled by placing the thumb under the fingers. Veckenstedt[39] and Laistner[40] say that whoever succeeds in pressing his big toe three times against the bedstead will frighten the Murawa away. All these suppositions arise from the observed fact that the nightmare disappears as soon as the sleeper recovers the lost capacity for movement by a slight motion of the fingers or toes.

The Greek physicians also observed regular epidemics of nightmares. Caelius Aurelianus writes: "Silimachus (an error for Callimachus) a pupil of Hippocrates, relates that many were carried away by this contagion just like the plague in the city of Rome." This obviously refers to the Hippocratic Callimachus, who was a pupil of Herophilus in the third or second century bce. The ancient writers, and in particular Soranus, emphasize that the nightmare can be considered a dangerous ailment only when it affects the same person time and again. Under these circumstances there may be chlorosis, emaciation, insomnia, constipation, and, if the attacks are especially violent and frequent, sometimes even epilepsy and death. Soranus believes that in *its* essence every nightmare is identical with an epileptic attack. (Even before the time of Soranus, the physician Rufus of Ephesus, explained the nightmare as a sign of incipient epilepsy.) The victims of a nightmare suffer while asleep exactly the same as does the epileptic while awake. Hence the evil must be dealt with energetically at its root so that the condition does not become chronic and permit the onset of epilepsy, mental disturbance, mania, or apoplexy. (Soranus describes epileptics as those who have heavy and appalling dreams and easily become insane.) As faithful pupils and followers of their great master Hippocrates, the ancient physicians strongly opposed the prevalent popular belief that the nightmare was a god or wicked spirit. Soranus in particular refutes this superstition in detail in his *Aetiology*. Caelius Aurelianus writes: "The above mentioned disease is however incipient epilepsy. Soranus explained fully convincingly in his books on the causes of disease, which he called *Aetiology,* that there is here neither a god nor a semi-god nor Cupid" (in error for concupiscence). I presume that Soranus is thinking here of erotic nightmares and of the teaching of Herophilus, according to which our concupiscence or our erotic instinct can produce dreams of this kind. Soranus considers even erotic nightmares as incipient epilepsy, especially since epileptic attacks are often associated with gonorrhoea without the erotic instinct (cupido) being present. As soon as the attack has passed and the victim is awake one can observe that the face and body orifices are covered with moist sweat, and the patient feels a heaviness in the nape of the neck and has a mild irritating cough. This cough is presumably only a natural sequel to the precedent dyspnea.

As regards the aetiology or cause of the nightmare, the ancients had already noted that it frequently originates from digestive upsets following overeating, alcoholic excesses, and eating indigestible food.

Naturally, the ancients knew nothing about its causation through mechanical obstruction of the respiratory inlets as first noted by Börner. Another feature correctly observed in ancient times was that the state of sleep-drunkenness or the transition period between fully asleep and fully awake is very favorable to the production of a nightmare; and that the visions of the dream may then persist so vividly for a period before falling asleep or after waking up that the sleeper will deceive himself into believing that he sees the vision with open eyes and in actual reality. Thus, for example, Macrobius, probably following one of the old physicians, writes:

> Fantasma is indeed a vision, between waking and deep sleep, in those first mists of sleep when one still believes oneself to be awake and has just fallen asleep, which seems to be forcing its way in as wandering forms of varying size, shape, or temper, either joyful or disturbing. Ephialtes is of this type, which popular belief holds to come in on the sleepers and weigh on them heavily and oppress them severely.[41]

More modern medical opinion confirms that deception of the senses often occurs in the state directly preceding sleep.

The fact that certain illnesses—especially those associated with hectic fever—produce a variety of terrifying nightmarish *visions* of vivid intensity was quite familiar to the ancient physicians. Let us compare, for example, Hippocrates: "The evil in these fevers and cramps (contortions) from dreams,"[42] to which Galen adds: "We also notice in dreadful illnesses oppressions, fears, and cramps stemming from dreams." Again Hippocrates: "Once he has gone to sleep he jumps up from his sleep when he sees the monstrous visions" (previously the talk was of fever). Later he continues: "Critias reports on feverish dreams." Galen: "I have called those who suffer from physical illnesses clear-sighted and those who are frightened by dreams prophets and seers through phantasmata."

From these fears, which according to Hippocrates also attack small children in their sleep (as noted above, the *pavores nocturni*), the god of dreams, Phobetor, obviously derives his name in Ovid's *Metamorphoses* and to him are ascribed in particular the production of all kinds of terrifying animal apparitions. The frightful and monstrous things, the confusion of the senses, the startled flight from the bed presumably also belong in this context, i.e., those night deliria and nightmares considered signs of epilepsy in the broader sense and which Hippocrates talks about in *The Sacred Disease*. We learn from Hippocrates that people believed them to be the influence of evil spirits of the dead against which one employed sacrifices of purification and expiation and incantations.

Even the layman had such frequent opportunity of witnessing nightmarish deliria and hallucinations during fever that it does not seem strange if sometimes the two conceptions of fever and nightmare are interchanged and the usual Ephialtes as the demon of the nightmare is repeatedly called Ipialos, Ipialis. Aristotle, in "On Dreams," acknowledged the close kinship between deliria and dreams when he wrote: "We meet the same symptoms in people startled from their dreams, as indeed dreams cause illnesses." Aristophanes is obviously thinking of severe fevers allied with dangerous dyspnea and nightmares and of their demons when he boasts that he fought as a second Hercules: "For you he fought, and for you he fights:/And then last year with adventurous hand/He grappled besides with the Spectral Shapes,/The Agues and Fevers that plagued our land."[43]

The remedies and dietetic discipline employed by the ancient doctors for nightmares were closely aligned with their views on their origin. The majority and most important of these remedies aimed at removing the damaging morbid humors and changing them into beneficial ones—corresponding to the basic theory of the humors in ancient medicine. The main therapy used was primarily venesection and various kinds of purgatives. One of these was a mixture of black hellebore and the juice of convolvulus with the addition of anise, caucus, and parsley. Another time-honored domestic remedy was the black pips of peony, which were employed against fears, demons, epilepsy, and cold fever, i.e., nightmares and deliria of all kinds. Galen recommended hellebore and venesection also for apoplexy, epilepsy, and melancholy. According to Dioscorus, a mixture of hellebore and scammony should be used as catharsis for epilepsy, melancholy, and insanity (delirium). In the vernacular the peony was even called Ephialtion. For effective dietetic treatment Soranus-Caelius advises several days of fasting and then an easily digestible simple diet, strictly avoiding all foodstuffs producing flatulence, above all beans. Beans were strictly forbidden to the Pythagoreans because they were considered to be very indigestible and causative of evil dreams and nightmares by their flatulent action. Plinius even reports a remarkable superstition according to which the "souls of the dead," i.e., evil spirits, were believed to dwell in beans.[44] This notion is immediately understandable if one remembers that evil spirits were believed to act personally in evil dreams, nightmares, and illnesses and to alarm and torment the sleeping or the sick with their appearances. Hence the belief that they dwell in certain injurious foods and that the intake of these foods would bring the spirits temporarily into the human body. The most important of these demons living in plants was Dionysus, the god of wine, ivy, and perhaps also of hemp, endowed with narcotic strength. He was directly identified with ivy and vine and, having transferred himself to men by their enjoyment of the produce of these plants, he animated and inspired, indeed possessed them.

We also meet the same—and probably a most ancient—popular superstition in Porphyrius. He observes on the demons causing nightmares that they enter into the human body with the food and there do all kinds of mischief and, in particular, bring on flatulence: "As we eat, they enter into us and settle in us and thus they pollute, not by divine interference. They generally delight in blood and filthiness and invade the possessed. In a word, a compulsion of greed and desire, and general excitation cloud rational thinking and unintelligible sounds connected with them and also flatulence cause man's breakdown which satisfies the demon."[45] It seems to be evident from the fragment found in Proclus that Porphyrius was probably thinking of the demons of vicious dreams and nightmares that live in certain unwholesome foods when speaking of the flatulence aroused by malevolent demons. Zeller has related this to the ancient beliefs about *incubi*.[46] The unintelligible sounds most probably refer not only to belches and flatulence but also to the inarticulate shrieks of the victim tormented by the nightmare.

The constituent elements of the apparition in the classical nightmare were approximately the same as in the modern one. In the classical era, too, the specter was sometimes terrifying, sometimes erotic, sometimes combining both characteristics; it revealed itself either in animal or in human form (male or female) or in a form part human, part animal. The most generally accepted concept about the essence of the spectre was that he or she was a wicked demon—particularly a malicious spirit of the dead—who intended to torture men in their sleep. Nevertheless, there was an ancient popular belief that wicked people like sorceresses and witches can also appear as nightmares. Finally, there occurs here and there the apparition of a kindly and benevolent nightmare spirit who renders useful service to man by curing him, revealing the future to him and bestowing treasures upon him. This becomes very evident from the following small collection of nightmares, that, incidentally, makes no claim to absolute completeness.

1. A he-goat appears as a nightmare spirit in the rhetorical novel of Iamblichu of which, unfortunately, only a far too brief outline has been preserved by Photius in his library: "A he-goat specter lusted after Sinonis; so they fled across the meadows of Rhodanis," i.e., the pair of lovers, Rhodanes and Sinonis, who form the center of the novel had escaped to a meadow from the persecution of the king of Babylon and were driven from the meadow by a nightmare demon in the form of a he-goat who assaulted the beautiful Sinonis in her sleep. Since Iamblichos was of Syrian extraction—and consequently Semitic—and brought up in Babylon, the he-goat is probably a so-called *sair,* i.e., one of the field ghosts or field devils related to the Pans, Satyrs, and Fauns who are mentioned repeatedly in the Old Testament. Mannhardt had previously conjectured this correctly.

2. Philostratus tells an exactly parallel story in the *Life of Apollonius of Tyana* (6.27), of an erotic nightmare spirit appearing in the form of a satyr. While Apollonius and his companions were staying in an Ethiopian village not far from the Nile cataracts and were eating their evening meal, they suddenly heard shouting by women who called out to one another, "Seize him and persecute him!" They also asked their husbands to punish the "adulterer." This village had been haunted for ten months by the ghost of a satyr who had evil designs on the women and was even said to have murdered two with whom he was particularly in love. (A similar love-demon, Asmodaius—from the Hebrew *Ashmedai,* the marriage-wrecker, "limping devil"—is mentioned in the Book of Tobias. He was in love with Sarah, the daughter of Raguel, and had killed her seven husbands one after another during their bridal nights. Tobias banished him into the desert by cremating the liver of a fish). The story continues to tell how Apollonius tamed and rendered harmless the demonic satyr by intoxicating him with wine—just as Midas did to the silenus (or satyr)—and banished him into a nymph grotto nearby. Philostratus adds a further parallel from his own experience when he says:

We must not disbelieve that satyrs both exist and are susceptible to the passion of love; for I knew a youth of my own age in Limnos whose mother was said to be visited by a satyr, as he well might to judge by this story; for he was represented as wearing on his back a fawnskin that exactly fitted him, the front paws of which were drawn around his neck and fastened over his chest.

Considering the frequent mixing of the concepts of Pan and Satyr (Faunus) in the Hellenistic age, one could in this case again think of Pan as the chief representative of the nightmare in the last centuries of the classical period.[47] The legend of the procreation of the sophist Apsines is probably based on a similar concept. One can assume that his mother imagined to have had intercourse with Pan in a dream and afterwards considered Apsines to be Pan's son, especially as he bore a certain resemblance to him. The story of Apollonius of Tyana as narrated by Philostratus is remarkable, by the way, in that a ten-months epidemic of nightmares should have prevailed among the women of the Ethiopian village; however, after the analogies quoted above this is by no means improbable.

3. A type of nightmare that we may deduce from Horace[48] has a completely different and nonerotic character. In these verses, an unfortunate boy who was ruthlessly murdered by a number of witch-like women to gain an effective love potion threatened his bloodthirsty murderesses just before his death with the following words:

As soon as you shall have satisfied your rage and I expire, my ghost shall haunt you every night. I will mangle your cheeks with my nails, for such is the power the manes give to specters; every night, I will wait round your beds, and incumbent on your troubled breasts, I will disturb your sleep by the most frightful appearances.

Obviously, the unfortunate victim is threatening his murderesses that after his death he will become a terrible ghost of the dead, a nightmare demon, and will wreak frightful vengeance upon them. (Compare Porphyrius: "The lemures, the shadows of the dead wandering at dawn, are to be feared."[49]) The nightmare is marked quite distinctly in the second and fifth lines—compare the "climbing up and settling on the chest" that Soranus (through Caelius) uses of the nightmare. The last line again finds an admirable explanation in Soranus where he says of the incubus: "Those who have suffered from the affliction for a long time are pale and thin because of their fear they do not get sleep." Plutarch also states that frightful dreams and nightmares usually end with a sudden awakening that is sometimes followed by very great psychic unrest. Line 3 of the epode presents much more of a problem; it seems to suggest a scratching or lacerating of the face by a being equipped with claws. Perhaps they can be explained by recollecting the "great claws" of the goddesses of fate in Hesiod,[50] the clawed feet of the harpies and sirens, and finally of the Etruscan Charon. As I have recently pointed out, the original concept of the vulture form of such demons of the dead has been retained in these claws. Compare also Gervase of Tilbury,[51] where in the chapter on "Witches and Nocturnal Specters," the lamias are interpreted as "lamiae from *laniando* = lacerate because they lacerate children." More on this subject is to be found in Grimm's *German Mythology*.

The same holds true for the Roman strixes, owlish demons with curved claws and beaks like vultures who lacerate the cheeks of children and eat their intestines as do vultures.[52] Compare also what Dinon in Pliny[53] tells of the Indian sirens: "They charm people with their song and when they are sunk in heavy sleep tear them to pieces." According to modern Greek superstition, the *kallikantzaroi* who belong to this type of demon also tear the face of those whom they meet during the night. I presume this motif is explained by the observation of a facial eruption that is called *epinuktis* and breaks out suddenly during the night. This occurs especially in children and is associated with severe nightmares.

Often victims appear to their murderers in dreams at night or in hallucinations when half awake but still drunk with sleep. They take the form of ghostly evil demons, terrify their victims and foretell their imminent destruction. An example is the ghost of the murdered Julius Caesar who appeared to Brutus and Cassius. Plutarch calls the ghost appearing to Brutus "your evil daemon." According to Valerius Maximus the same is true for the "man of enormous size, black in color, with filthy beard and unkempt hair" who terrified Gaius Cassius Parmensis shortly before his death "in the first sleep, when he lay on his couch asleep with anxiety and troubles."[54] In both cases the evil daemon can only be Caesar himself or his personal genius. What is described is most probably a nightmare, and yet some of the most characteristic signs are missing: jumping up, rushing in, burdening, weighing down; likewise in the dreadful dream of Aulus Caecina in Tacitus.[55]

4. In the very dramatically depicted nightmare in Apuleius,[56] there are two witches who appear to the unhappy Aristomenes while he is asleep and torment him in the most appalling manner. It is possible that the concept lying at the basis of this dream is similar to that found in many Nordic sagas, i.e., that the soul of the living possess the power of leaving the body during sleep and of appearing to others in their dreams, thereby imparting a kind of reality. (I am referring to the Norse *fylgja*.) After a sumptuous evening meal, filled abundantly with meat and drink, Aristomenes went to bed together with his friend Socrates. The latter fell at once into a deep sleep. Aristomenes, however, bolted the door securely and placed his own bed against it for further protection. When he had at last gone to sleep, the door sprang open with a mighty crash and enormous force. This overthrew the bed, and the sleeper came to rest underneath it. At the same time two old witches entered and pierced his sleeping friend with a sword, drew his blood, and closed the wound with a sponge. After this the two witches attacked Aristomenes who was covered with cold sweat from fright. They dragged him from under his bed and "straddling over my face they emptied their bladders and drenched me with the foulest urine." (The modern Greek *kallikantzaroi,* who are in many ways related to the Pans and Satyrs, act in a similar fashion.) In this classical nightmare we find once more nearly all the characteristics that were regarded as specific to the nightmare by the ancient physicians: the nightmare originated from indigestible food, there was profuse sweating, particularly on the face (Soranus through Caelius: "Then, when they awake from sleep, the face and the parts used in swallowing feel moist and humid"), which then led to the disgusting impression of the two witches urinating on his face. Furthermore, the feeling of pressure and being strangled is excellently motivated by the overturned bed on top of the sleeper and the two women sitting on his face. Finally there is the dreadful condition and fright of the unhappy sleeper when he wakes up, which is dramatically described: "Lifeless, naked, and cold and covered with urine, as if but recently emerged from the maternal womb, or rather half dead."

5. In his story of Demaratus, King of Sparta, Herodotus[57] describes a remarkable erotic nightmare, which is mythologically of special importance because a large number of fables about birth can be explained on this analogy. When Leotychidas, his adversary, reproached Demaratus

that he was not the real son of the king Ariston, since the king himself had cast doubts on his paternity, Demaratus charged his mother in the most solemn manner to tell him the whole truth of his origin. His mother replied:

> On the third night after Ariston had brought me to his house, there came to me an appearance like to Ariston, and lay with me, and then put on me the garlands which he had. So when that figure was gone, presently Ariston came to me. Seeing the garlands on me, he asked me who had given them. I said they were his gift, but he denied it. Then I said, and swore it, that he did not well to deny it; for I told him he had come but a little while ago and lain with me and so given me the garlands. When Ariston saw that I swore to that, he perceived that the hand of heaven was in the matter; and not only were the garlands plainly seen to have come from the hero shrine they call Astrabacus's shrine, that stands by the door of the courtyard, but the diviners declared that it was that same hero, Astrabacus, that had visited me. Thus, my son, you have all that you desire to know. For either you are the son of that hero, and the hero Astrabacus is your father, or Ariston is, for on that night did I conceive you.

(The same motif is found in the medieval legend of Robert the Devil.)

The fable is important for us as it comes from historic times. It is clearly transmitted and has a number of analogies from historical and mythological times. Here the tradition about Alexander the Great comes to mind, whose mother Olympias is said to have conceived him during a dream in which Zeus appeared in the form of lightning. Then there are the supernatural births of Plato, Seleucus, and Augustus and the Thasian legend about the birth of Theagenes; finally the fables concerning Zeus and Alcmene, Zeus and Danae, Zeus and Semele, Mars and Ilia, etc. Even today the impulse to fable similar legends has not fully died. The following extract from Pashley throws a light on folklore traced in Crete:

> A *katakhanás* [i.e., a malevolent death demon = vampire] appeared in Anópolis, plagued the people, and raped a woman. He induced the men to leave their wives, called some other vampires, and made the women believe they were their husbands. When one of the men came and asked, "What is wrong with you?" The wife answered, "You have used me clumsily and frequently." The man, however, said, "It was not I who came." And the wife retorted, "Then it was a vampire." Later they banished the vampire by exorcism onto the island of Santorin.[58]

In the Middle Ages, the ancient heroes, demons, and gods who mingled with man in erotic nightmares naturally became devils. They appear sometimes as *incubi,* sometimes as *succubi,* and occasionally father children who afterwards become evil sorcerers, witches, etc. This concept plays a large part in proceedings against witches. Goethe's poem *The Bride of Corinth* shows what a high poetical understanding and representation is capable of. The poem is based on Phlegon of Tralles's story of a vampire in his *Book of Marvels.*

6. We meet yet another type of erotic nightmare in the interesting Hellenic relief for which we are indebted to Crusius's "The Epiphany of the Siren."[59] A beautiful, voluptuous siren with half-stretched wings and human legs which terminate in pointed falcon-like claws is lowering herself onto a shepherd or peasant apparently asleep in the open air and is obviously showing erotic intentions. (Compare Josephus: "During the night Matthew appeared to have intercourse with a woman in a dream,"[60] and primarily the sculptures showing the sphinx attacking a recumbent youth, where the monster may signify a nightmare demon.) Crusius points out correctly that in Hellenistic literature—which must be cited to understand the imagery—the sirens were believed to be the daughters of Achelous and a muse, rather akin to the Naiads, and according to Dinon in Pliny,[61] these sirens "charm people with their song, and when they are sunk in heavy sleep, tear them to pieces." The Naiads were also reputed to be daughters of the river gods and especially of Achelous. We find similar beliefs about the North German elves. These are also distinguished by their beauty and like to bask in the sunshine. (Our siren is also a southern demon.) If a female elf wishes to unite herself with a man, she flies to him on a sunbeam through some opening such as a keyhole or a crack in the room—exactly like the nightmare demons. It is dangerous to approach her hillock, and many a youth who has gone to sleep on an elves' hillock has never returned to his companions (this is also true of the nymphs). The elves are fond of dancing on meadows in moonlight nights. Corresponding to the elves dancing on moonlit meadows are the sirens as playmates of Persephone as she picks flowers in the fields. A blow from an elf causes lameness or brings on illness. The elves shoot their arrows down through the air, and similarly the elf's "shot" carries death. The same holds true for nymphs. In Icelandic folklore the elves have love affairs with human beings. Closely connected with the

elves are the vampire-like Empusae and Lamiae of whom it is said in Philostratus: "These beings fall in love, and they are devoted to the delights of Aphrodite but especially to the flesh of human beings. And they decoy with such delights those whom they mean to devour in their feasts."[62] Let us take this opportunity to recall the *insomnia Veneris* or *somni Venerei* (bad dreams of Venus) that are so closely allied pathologically with nightmares. These are erotic dreams associated with gonorrhea, and the doctors in ancient times believed them to be the precursors or symptoms of epilepsy and insanity—just as with nightmares. The people also attributed them to the powers of daemons.

7. An obvious nightmare or nightmare vision is portrayed in Genesis. Here it is written:

> That same night [Jacob] got up and took his two wives, his two maids, and his eleven children, and crossed the ford of the Jabbok. He took them and sent them across the stream, and likewise everything that he had. Jacob was left alone; and a man wrestled with him until daybreak. When the man saw that he did not prevail against Jacob, he struck him on the hip socket; and Jacob's hip was put out of joint as he wrestled with him. Then he said, "Let me go, for the day is breaking." But Jacob said, "I will not let you go, unless you bless me." So he said to him, "What is your name?" And he said, "Jacob." Then the man said, "You shall no longer be called Jacob, but Israel: for you have striven with God and with humans, and you have prevailed." Then Jacob asked him, "Please tell me your name." But he said, "Why is it that you ask my name?" And there he blessed him. So Jacob called the place Peniel, saying, "For I have seen God face to face, and yet my life is preserved." The sun rose upon him as he passed Peniel, limping because of his hip. Therefore to this day the Israelites do not eat the thigh muscle that is on the hip socket, because he struck Jacob on the hip socket at the thigh muscle. (Genesis 32: 22–32).

The notion that mortals who see God against God's will must die or become blind is widespread. One thinks of Actaeon, Semele, Tiresias, etc. Even if in this remarkable legend of Elohim it is not explicitly stated that the nocturnal struggle between Jacob and Elohim is to be interpreted as a dream or a nightmare, there can scarcely be any doubt after all the evidence has been taken into consideration, and any other interpretation, such as a violent struggle in prayer or an actual reality, is unthinkable. Most of the more recent commentators on Genesis look upon Jacob's struggle with Elohim as a work of fiction or a myth; yet they abstain from a scientific interpretation and, strange to say, reject the earlier opinion that the struggle is to be construed as a dream. When Dillmann says that

> the wrestling with God as understood by the legend, was a physical occurrence in the material world. The statement about Jacob's limping (verse 32) is more than sufficient to establish this. It is only entire misapprehension which can "explain the occurrence as something purely subjective, such as a vivid dream, or a fervent wrestling with God in prayer"...[63]

he pays no attention to the fact that vivid nightmares often appear to the sleeper as objective external experiences, and he does not heed the fact that all the motives contained in the legend—for example, the paralysis of the hip—recur in nightmares, as will be pointed out in the following. The fact that the struggle in question is not specifically designated as a dream experience must not be considered an obstacle, for dreams, and especially nightmares, which have been conspicuous by their peculiar vividness, have frequently not been recognized as dreams, but have been described as factual experiences. As we have already seen, even modern physicians accustomed to accurate observation of themselves, have sometimes mistaken subjective dream phenomena of great intensity for real experiences. Let us compare, for example, in the *Odyssey,* where Ulysses, hidden in the form of an eagle, appears to Penelope in a dream and calls out to her: "This is not a dream but a happy reality that you shall see fulfilled." One thinks also of the remarkable story of the cure of Sostrata of Pherae,[64] where it is reported how this patient had set out on her return journey without having received a clear vision in a dream and on the way was cured by Asclepius when she was fully awake and not through the agency of a dream. A charming ode of Horace[65] is based on a similar dream vision. The best analogy of all, however, is furnished by the nightmare of Hyginus,[66] which is expressly stated to be a real experience. Furthermore there is the not unimportant fact that the Elohist to whom we are indebted for our legend also makes God reveal himself in dreams elsewhere. If we now look at the story more accurately, we can see in point of fact that all the motives found in this legend are also found in dreams, and especially in nightmares, and in the myths derived from them.Thus we can see primarily the motive of the night struggle and this, according to Artemidorus, not only happens frequently in dreams but also plays a role in undoubted nightmares. The words to be specially noticed in Artemidorus are: "The dream, which brings victory to one of the two wrestlers, who keeps his strength until the break of dawn."[67] According to Artemidorus, "a struggle with an unknown opponent means danger through illness," and this is certainly true of Jacob who acquired a paresis of the hip from the struggle with the stranger. Thus, for example, Veckenstedt tells us the following story about the Slavic nightmare demon Serpolnica: "A woman went out late in the evening to cut grass and did not hear the clock strike twelve. She was assaulted by Serpolnica and struggled with her for a full hour until it struck one o'clock, when the ghost left her. She returned to her home completely exhausted and dishevelled."[68] We shall see later that wood ghosts often appear as nightmare demons, as for example the Celtic Dusii and the Italic Silvanus and Faunus. Similarly, Veckenstedt in his *Lithuanian Myths* says of the Lithuanian Medine or forest woman: "It can happen to whoever goes through the wood that the Medine forces him to struggle with her; should he be victorious he is richly rewarded," (as Jacob was by the blessing!) "but if he is defeated, she devours him." Kolrusch[69] and Perty[70] say that the nightmare is sometimes so intense that the sleeper contending with the specter tumbles out of his bed; obviously the fall may cause sprains, laming, and all kinds of injuries.

A second nightmare motif can be seen in the duration of the struggle up to daybreak and in the request of Elohim to the victorious Jacob to release him because dawn is breaking; for it is one of the characteristics of night demons and specters that they are linked with night and darkness and that they have to escape if either a light is kindled or if day breaks.[71] The first ray of daylight banishes the night demons,[72] or if the first cockcrow is heard heralding the break of day. The crowing of the cock proclaims that it is day and frightens the spirits away (Grimm). This view is also expressed in Parsi teaching and in the Talmud. In proof of this I refer to the following Lithuanian legend communicated by Veckenstedt.[73] It relates to the Caucie, small nightmare demons with long grey beards who glide into the room to throttle the sleeper when the moon is full:

> A peasant who was often plagued by them asked his neighbors for advice, and afterwards he lit a torch as soon as he noticed that the Caucie had come. Thereupon they avoided him because the bright light frightened them. Another peasant in like circumstances

bought three cocks on the advice of the parish priest. He kept these cocks constantly awake so that they crowed during the night, too. During the next night the Caucie had scarcely begun to torment him when the cocks crowed, and the Caucie disappeared.

Moreover, the fact that Jacob asked Elohim his name and that Elohim did not wish to divulge it, points decidedly to a nightmare. In Germanic superstition you must call the demon by his name if you are going to capture him, i.e., get him into your power.[74] "For protection against witches in the form of animals (who often act as nightmare demons) and to force them to resume their human form again, they must be called three times by their Christian name." The witches then usually appear naked. Compare also Grohmann in *Aberglauben und Gebräuche aus Böhmen und Mähren*: "When the haunted person addresses the animal form (of the nightmare) squatting on him by the name of the person who is causing the nightmare in the metamorphosis of the animal, the person will stand before him in his or her human form and cannot hurt him any more."[75] A sentence in Bühler's *Davos in seinem Walserdialekt* runs: "If you know the name of a *Doggi* (nightmare specter) or of a *Fänken,* you have him in your power."[76] The same belief exists among the Slavic Wends whose nightmare demon is called Murawa. In this context Laistner writes: "If you can more or less conjecture who it is you feel to be lying upon you (as a nightmare demon) you must call him by his name, and the Murawa will escape."[77] This motif plays a big part in numerous fairytales and saga collected by Laistner. The best known is that of Rumpelstilzkin.

When it is further said in the Genesis legend that Jacob acquired a dislocation (that is to say, a paresis) of the hip from his struggle with Elohim, this motif can be accounted for without difficulty from the scope of nightmares. In the first place the rheumatic pains contracted by slumbering incautiously in the open air and known as witch or demon "shots" spring to mind. This designation clearly shows that such pains and pareses were ascribed by the people to the beings who became visible in nightmares.[78] The "blow" of the Greek Nereids is a similar belief. This was directed particularly against people who went to sleep about midday in a lonely spot in the open air near springs and streams and manifested itself by mental or physical illness. Note that the laming of Jacob took place on the bank of the river Jabbok where the cold exhalations during the night—due to the steep fall in temperature—could produce rheumatic lameness. Finally the Brandenburg nightmare demon Scherber (*Serp, Serpel*) falls into this category. This is the male counterpart of Serpolnica and hacks the plagued victim in the heel with a curved knife (sickle?), just as in the Austrian alplands it is considered highly dangerous to tread barefoot into the footprints of the *Hafergeiss* when this demon goat appears as a nightmare devil, because one immediately feels the *Gallschuss* (a shot of bile), which produces a piercing pain in the foot as caused by rheumatism or gout.[79]

Finally, there only remains to prove that the blessing that Jacob forced the defeated Elohim to bestow on him is also a motif of the nightmare dream. To make this comprehensible I refer once more to the Lithuanian Medine or forest woman who compels anyone going through the woods to wrestle with her, and if the person is victorious, he is richly rewarded, but if he is defeated, she devours him. Very frequently the victory over the nightmare demon consists in the person seizing the spirit's cap and compelling the demon to grant or divulge a treasure—a concept that Petronius knew when he said about a penniless man who had suddenly become rich by some mysterious means: "He who has robbed the incubus of a hair finds a treasure."[80] This motif is found in numerous Italian, modern Greek, Germanic, and Slavic sagas from which I shall narrate only the following characteristic one. Among the Sandomier forest dwellers the nightmare demon is called the *Vjek* ("old man") or *Gnotek* ("small oppressor"). Nobody knows where he spends his days. He is not big but exceedingly heavy. The *Vjek* lies down on an unsuspecting sleeper and compresses his chest with all his strength so that the victim cannot move. People say that if anyone can snatch away the *Vjek's* cap, the *Vjek* will bring him plenty of money.

The blessing that the nightmare demon confers may also consist in the communication of important and useful secrets or in the granting of strength and good health. As we shall see later, this feature of blessing, of doing good and being of service, is imprinted and developed to an exceptional degree in the Germanic domestic spirits (*spiritus familiares*) who are at the same time nightmare demons. Thus the connection between the hitherto unexplained name of Mephistopheles and Ophelis/Epophelis ("helper, benefactor") becomes clear since he was one of these useful domestic spirits according to the old Faust legend.

8. The view mentioned above of a health-promoting and blessing-bestowing field of activity of the nightmare demon is expressed in an epigram in Kaibel, which has been variously misunderstood. This inscription was found in Rome, and Kaibel dates it about the second century CE. In it, a shepherd claims to have been cured of a serious illness by the appearance of Pan-Ephialtes while he was taking his midday rest. The epigram runs:

> To you, o flute player, hymnist, benevolent god
> Pure leader of the Naiads pouring bath waters,
> Hyginus, whom you yourself healed of severe illness
> by coming near him, presents this oblation.
> For you have appeared to all my sheep,
> not as a dream vision but in the middle of the day.[81]

Compare this to Artimidorus where the same antithesis of dream and day is found, and of course the Odyssey where Ulysses calls to Penelope in a dream, "Take heart, daughter of the noble Icarius. This is not a dream but a happy reality you shall see fulfilled."

Almost all scholars who have reviewed this interesting inscription hold the opinion that the godhead who is presented with the oblation is Apollo-Paean although nowhere else is he called soriktis ("flute player"). Plew and Drexler are the only writers who have connected the epigram correctly with Pan, who is elsewhere, as here, called hymnist, leader of the Naiads, and flute player, as Drexler correctly noted. Furthermore, the fact that Pan[82] reveals himself in dreams to people during their midday sleep—just as here—justifies this interpretation. In Longus,[83] all kinds of terrifying day and night visions are interpreted as "revelations of Pan's anger with the sailors." We advance further in the understanding of our epigram by the insight that the instance of Hygeinus does not—as Plew and Robert assume—deal with an ordinary dream but is rather one of those vivid nightmares that, as we have just seen, were attributed to Pan-Ephialtes and according to ancient popular belief were said to have curative effects on illness. Pan—like Asclepius—healed the sick through dreams:

> On going down from here you come to a sanctuary of Pan Lyterius...
> so named because he showed to the Troezenian magistrates dreams
> that supplied a cure for the epidemic that had afflicted Troezenia
> and the Athenians more than any other people.[84]

Nightmares may well be concerned in this case as well, for, as we shall see later, they correspond better with the nature of Pan than do ordinary dreams. Drexler believes this is not a nightmare but a vision experienced while awake, because it states expressly that the god appeared to Hygeinus "not as a dream vision but in the middle of the day." I, however, wish to point out that the notions of dream and vision intermingle in many ways, and nightmares are often so vivid that they can be confused with real experiences even by experienced physicians. The facts at the basis of our epigram are most probably these: a shepherd, Hygeinus, is afflicted with a severe physical complaint and about mid-day lies down to rest among his flock. While he believes that he is still awake, Pan-Ephialtes (the god of both shepherds and hunters) appears to him in an exceedingly vivid dream and by this apparition cures him. The same is true of the incubation dreams in which the god, demon, or hero who lives physically in the temple appears to the dreamer and cures him either by personal intervention or by telling him the therapy. The vividness of the dream sometimes reaches the pitch where the sleeper believes that he has seen the awearance of the god when awake and not when asleep. This is evident in the remarkable story of the cure of Sostrata in the second catalogue of Epidaurus.

In accepting a physical and not simply dreamed apparition of the god, Hygeinus is strengthened by the fact that at the same time his animals fell victims to a panicky terror (likewise attributed to the god), and out of gratitude he offers an oblation to the rescuing god for having been cured. Perhaps Pan's appellative Paean relates to him in his capacity as helper and saviour, as the rescuer from illness. The representation of Ephialtes as a rescuing and redeeming healing god is easily explained by the feeling of rescue and redemption following most nightmares. We shall see later that nightmare and panicky terror are closely related concepts and are therefore frequently assigned to the same demons.

35. Caelius Aurelianus, *De morbis chronicis* I, cap. 3, ed. J.C. Amman (Amsterdam, 1722), 288.

36. Ibid.

37. L. Laistner, *Das Rätsel der Sphinx: Grundzüge einer Mythengeschichte* (Berlin: Verlag von Wilhelm Hertz, 1889), 1: 41, 52–53.

38. A. Wuttke, *Der deutsche Volksaberglaube der Gegenwart* (Berlin: Verlag von Wiegandt & Grieben, 1900), par. 419.

39. *Wendische Sagen, Märchen und abergläubische Gebräuche*, ed. E. Vecken-stedt (Graz: Verlag von Leuschner & Lubensky, 1880), 131.

40. Laistner, *Das Rätsel der Sphinx*, 2:230.

41. Macrobius, *Commentarii in Somnium Scipionis*, 1.3.7.

42. Hippocrates, *Aphorisms*, 3.736, K.

43. Aristophanes, *Vespae*, 1037ff.

44. Pliny (the Elder), *Naturalis Historia*, 18.18.

45. Porphyrius, *De Philosophia ex Oraculis Haurienda*, ed. Wolff, 149.

46. E. Zeller, *Die Philosophie der Griechen in ihrer geschichtlichen Entwick-lung* (Tübingen: Verlag von Ludwig Friedrich Fues, 1852), 3.2:604.

47. Cf. A. Furtwängler, *Der Satyr aus Pergamon* (Berlin: G. Reimer, 1880), 30ff.

48. Horace, *Epodi*, 5.91ff.

49. Porphyrius, *De Philos. ex Orac. Haur.*, 2.2.209.

50. Hesiod, *Aspis*, 254.

51. Gervase of Tilbury, *Otia Imperialia*, 39.

52. Ovid, *Fasti*, 6.134.

53. Pliny (the Elder), *Naturalis Historia*, 10.136.

54. Valerius Maximus, 1.7.7.

55. Flavius Josephus, *Antiquitates Judaicae*, 1.65.

56. Apuleius, Metamorphoses, 1.11ff.

57. Herodotus, 6.65ff.

58. R. Pashley, *Travels in Crete* (London: John Murray, 1837), II: 221.

59. O. Crusius, "Die Epiphanie der Sirene," *Philologus: Zeitschrift für das klassische Altertum* 50 (1891): 93–107.

60. Flavius Josephus, *Antiquitates Judaicae*, 17.6.4.

61. Pliny (the Elder), *Naturalis Historia*, 20.136.

62. Philostratus, *Vita Apollonii*, 4.25.

63. A. Dillmann, *Genesis: Critically and Exegetically Expounded*, trans. W.B. Stevenson (Edinburgh: T & T. Clark, 1897), 2:281.

64. Stele II at Epidaurus (testimony 25), in *Asclepius: Collection and Interpretation of the Testimonies*, ed. E. and L. Edelstein (Baltimore: The Johns Hopkins University Press, 1998), 1:234.

65. Horace, *Carmina*, 11.19.

66. G. Kaindl, *Epigrammata Graeca ex lapidipus conlecta* (Berlin: G. Reimer, 1878), no. 802.

67. Artemidorus, *Oneirocritica*, 1.60.

68. *Die Mythen, Sagen und Legenden der Zamaiten (Litauer)*, ed. E. Vecken-stedt (Heidelberg: Carl Winter's Universitätsbuchhandlung, 1883), 2:109.

69. C. Kohlrusch, *Schweizerisches Sagenbuch* (Leipzig: Rob. Hofmann, 1854), 318.

70. M. Perty, *Die mystischen Erscheinungen der menschlichen Natur* (Leipzig and Heidelberg: C.F. Winter'sche Verlagsbuchhandlung, 1872), 1:140.

71. Wuttke, *Der deutsche Volksaberglaube,* par. 772.

72. In Gottfried August Bürger's ballad "Lenore," verse 28.

73. *Die Mythen, Sagen und Legenden der Zamaiten (Litauer),* 2:145ff.

74. Wuttke, *Der deutsche Volksaberglaube,* par. 404.

75. Ibid., 415.

76. V. Bühler, *Davos in seinem Walserdialekt* (Heidelberg: n.p., 1870), 1:365.

77. Laistner, Das Rätsel der Sphinx, 1:41ff.

78. J. Grimm, *Deutsche Mythologie* (Göttingen: Dieterichsche Buchhandlung, 1835), 381.

79. *Mythen und Sagen Tirols,* ed. J.N. von Alpenburg (Zurich: Meyer und Zeller, 1857), 385; Laistner, Das Rätsel der Sphinx, 1:334.

80. Petronius, *Satyricon,* 38.

81. R.F. Kaindl, "Zauberglaube bei den Huzulen," *Globus* 76 (1899), no. 802.

82. Longus, *Pastorales,* 2.26.

83. Ibid., 2.25.

84. Pausanius, *Description of Greece,* 2.32.6. (trans. W.H.S. Jones).

3

The Old Designations of the Nightmare

We have by now become sufficiently acquainted with the nature and working of nightmares and nightmare demons to be able to understand their multiplicity of names etymologically, and we can therefore pass on to a short enumeration and investigation of these.

1. The two most widely known words for the nightmare are *epialtes* and *ephialtes*, which are related phonetically like *epiorkos* and *ephiorkos*. Another form seems to be present in the name of the Lycian *epaltes* (*Iliad*, 2.415). Alcaeus is said to have used the unaspirated form; otherwise it is considered to be Ionic and sometimes Attic. Moeris considers *epialtes* and *ephialtes* to be Hellenic forms in contradistinction to *tiphus*, which he declares to be Attic. The name of the notorious traitor in Herodotus is Epialtes; a vase from Kea bearing a representation of the giants' struggle shows the name of a giant, which on Attic vases and in the literature is sounded Ephialtes and is written as Hipialtes. Kretschmer derives this name from *iallo* (*hiallo*) and believes that the painter had written or wished to write Hepialtes. As to the significance of this, the ancient and the modern scholars vacillate between the derivations *iallo* ("I send," "I shoot") and *hallomai*. Phonetically both derivatives seem equally valid, but for content *hallesthai* is to be preferred because on the one hand *hallesthai* corresponds much more than *iallein* to the meaning of the verbs used elsewhere for the entrance of the nightmare, such as *epipiptein* (*pedan*), *irruere*, *invadere*, *incumbere*, *epherpein*, *eperchesthai*. The name given to the nightmare by the Romans was *incubo* (*-us*) from *incumbere* ("to lay oneself upon, to rush upon, to throw one's weight upon"). The name of the giant Ephialtes is obviously derived from *ephallesthai* ("to leap upon," to overpower") since Philostratus in *Life of Apollonius* (5.16) says of the giants "that they scaled the heaven and chased away the gods therefrom" (trans. F.C. Conybeare). On the other hand, it is employed elsewhere in a similar manner, just as of the nightmare, to describe the quick and sudden attacks of the warriors in Homer or to portray the

lightning descent of the bird of prey on its booty. Indeed, it even allows of a meaning of *ephallesthai,* corresponding to the erotic character of Ephialtes. Homer uses it in this sense in the *Odyssey* when speaking of Ulysses impetuously embracing and kissing his old father.

2. Likewise the rarer forms of *epi-al-es,* gen. *-etos, epi-al-os, iphi-al-os,* and *epi-al-tos* may be derived from *hallesthai.* For *epiales*—as testified by Hesychius of Alexandria and Georgius Choeroboscus—one is referred to a fragment of Sophron of Syracuse that runs: *Epiales ho ton patera pnigon* ("Epiales strangled his father"). Since we are ignorant of the context, it must unfortunately remain doubtful whether the nightmare demon Epiales is to be considered as strangling his own father or the father of another. In the latter instance, it could perhaps be taken for granted that the nightmare demon was originally a godless man and patricide who after his death became a tormenting strangler spirit. (When Aristophanes says in the Wasps, speaking of the *epialoi* and *pureloi,* "who strangled the fathers in the night and choked the grandfathers," and at the same time indicates that he, as a second Hercules, conquered these fiends, this could be an allusion to the position of Sophron or to these sources.) Alcaeus is said to have used *epialos* as closely connected with *epialtes.* Regarding the clearly active sense of the suffixes *-tos* in *epial-tos,* I would refer the reader to Raphael Kühner's *Ausführliche Grammatik der griechischen Sprache* (Hannover, 1835) and Gustav Meyer's *Griechische Grammatik* (Leipzig, 1880). Only with hesitation do I venture to name in this connection the form *epiales* mentioned by Hesychius, possibly instead of *epialles.* Moritz Schmidt (*Hesychii Alexandrini Lexicon*) prefers to read it either as *epialtes* or *epiales.*

3. The forms *epialos* and *epiales* are more difficult to elucidate. The most important entry on them is found in the *Etymologicum Magnum: epialos, epiales,* and epioles mean the agues of fever that also attack the sleepers as demons. Euphemistically *epios* is called "Tender One," "Friendly One." Apollonius, however, says that *epialtes* is called *epiales,* even with the *a* changing into *o—epioles.* The following extract from Eustathios shows that these words originate from Herodian: "In the writings of Herodian appears *epiales epialetos,* who, as he says, is used similarly by Sophron when Heracles strangles Epiales." From these scripts we can learn that on the one hand the shivering fit *rhigorpuretos,* as well as the nightmare and its demon, are designated by the same terms

epialos, epiales, and *epioles.* On the other hand, it is clear that the words *kat'antiphrasin* were derived from *epios,* i.e., were thought to have originated from the striving for euphemism. The duplicate meaning of *epialos* and *epiales* ("shivering fit" and "nightmare") can easily be explained from the above mentioned fact that nightmares frequently occur during fever deliria. (One should mention here the Paione—also called *epialteion*—which is said to be an equally effective remedy for both nightmares and agues.) However, it must for the time being be left undecided whether these words really are related to *epios* and can be traced back to an euphemism. It certainly is not inconceivable that the dreaded demon of fevers and nightmares was given a pleasant sounding name. One need only recall such euphemisms as "hospitable sea" in place of "inhospitable sea," "friendly night" for "deadly night," "auspicious" for "ominous" or "left" (unlucky signs come from the left), Eumenides ("gracious ones") for Erinyes ("Furies," literally "avengers"), and so on. One may hold the view that in the suffixes *-alos* and *-ales,* the *-al-* is identical with the root of *hallomai* ("to jump upon") and thus points to the *Hepi-al-os* and *Hepi-al-es* as a daimon *epios ephallomenos,* and thus perhaps the apparently identical parallel forms of *Epi-al-os* and *Epi-al-es* (see above) may have contributed considerably to this idea. In extracts of Greek verse there are several undoubted demons in the form of animals, and I think it probable that in *epaphos* we should see an animal demon, the hoopoe bird.

By far the most important fact we learn from Eustathius of Thessalonica is the myth contained in the fragment of Sophron from which it appears that Hercules was haunted by the nightmare (and fever?) demon; he repaid like with like by throttling this fiend just as the fiend had attempted to throttle him. We must perceive in this otherwise forgotten legend a parallel to the struggle—handed down only in ancient sculpture—of Hercules with Gyas (Geras), the personification of old age, or with Thanatos in the *Alcestes* of Euripides. Possibly the myth of Epiales and Hercules is represented on the cameo in C.W. King's *Antique Gems and Rings.* This is in a beautiful, severe style and has remained unexplained hitherto. Hercules sits in the position of a completely exhausted man or a man dropping off to sleep. His head and chest are bent far forwards, he is sitting on a stone (?) with his right hand leaning on his club. Approaching him from behind—it would seem furtively—is a powerful bearded man with large wings who holds a branch of a tree or a poppy stalk in his left hand, and to all appearances, snatches at the hero's throat with his right as if to throttle him. (Compare the definition of Epiales as a demon who creeps up to the sleepers or attacks them.) Similarly, Hypnos also frequently appears in sculptures as a bearded demon. He usually stands behind the sleeper, or less frequently, steps up to him pouring out sleep from a horn. Sometimes he touches the temples of the sleepy person with a twig or poppy stalk moistened with the dew of Lethe. He is frequently winged. It need scarcely be mentioned that the demon of the nightmare, working only in sleep or the state preceding sleep, or the demon of fever accompanied by restless, fearful dreams (*epialos, Epiales*), must have had a great deal in common with Hypnos (and Oneiros) from the first.

4. Just as was the demon of fever and shivering fits, the demon of typhoid fever (*tuphos, tuphomanie, tuphodes puretos*), which is often associated with raving delirium, confused sensual dreams (nightmares), intoxication, and stupor, also seems to have been identified or confused with the nightmare demon Ephialtes. (The sensuous dreams are probably connected with the emissions of semen, which Hippocrates had already observed in certain forms of typhoid.) Clearly Typhos, which signifies smoke or fumes, must denote an allied illness, sometimes accompanied by delirium and sometimes by heavy stupor, which in both symptoms is similar to the condition of those who have remained in smoke for a long time and who finally, if not rescued, must be suffocated by it. Smoke incidentally has the same effect on animals as on man. During the fire in October 1899 in the carnivore house of the Berlin Zoological Gardens, the animals were first infuriated by the smoke but then became quiet and stupefied rather quickly, and it was only with difficulty that they were aroused from this state.

The use of *tuphoo* (which means basically "to surround with smoke") is in complete harmony with this concept, because Hesychius explains *tetuphosthai* ("full of smoke") by *memenenai* ("rage"), *tetuphotai* ("full of fumes") by *embebrontetai* ("dumbfounded"); *tuphosai* ("to fill with smoke") by *pnixai* ("suffocate"), *apolesai* ("destroy"); and by *tetuphomenos* we understand a narcotized, foolish, irresponsible person. I should like to derive from tuphus ("smoke," "fume," "typhoid fever") tiphus as equal to Ephialtis, as is testified to by Didymus, Moeris, Photius, and Hesychius. That is, I assume that *tiphus* stands for the older *tuphus,* just as *phi-tu-s* stands for *phu-tus* and *phituo* for *phutuo*, because, according to Greek phonology, where two "u"s follow each other the first "u" often changes into an "i" by dissimilation. The ending -*us* seems to correspond to the usual -*eus*, as is seen from a number of vase inscriptions collected by Kretschmer—for example, *Nerus = Nereus*, *Tudus = Tudeus*, *Oinus = Oineus*, *Thesus = Theseus*—and from names occurring in literature like *Hippus = Hippeus* and *Nikus = Nikeus*. For that matter, it would also be possible to deduce *Tiph-us* ("nightmare") directly from *Tuphus* ("smoke," "fumes") and to assume that the "choking dream" (*Sticktraum*) or *pnigalion* owes its name *tiphus* to the effect of the smoke that, according to Börner, produces attacks of choking in sleeping people and therefore most probably nightmares. In this instance *tiphus* would signify the smoke dream (*Rauchtraum*). It is easy to think that in view of the poor quality of fire and lighting equipment in the classical period—especially in earliest times—poisoning by smoke and instances of stupor and nightmares (*tuphoi*) were exceedingly common, and every and anybody had frequent opportunity of observing these upon themselves and others.

5. The word *epheles* ("a ghostly being") was twice attested by Hesychius and considered by him as Aolic. It should probably be derived from the verb *eph-el-ein*, which means "to seize or attack." It would seem therefore to signify "attacker" and to mean the nightmare demon as the one who seizes the sleeper by the throat or closes his mouth so that the sensation of suffocation arises. We may recall in this context the Homeric *helon epi mastaka chersin ouk ea eipemenai*, which expresses Ulysses holding Eurycleia's mouth tightly shut. A similar presentation forms the basis for the use of *epilambanein* (compare *epilepsia*), which is often used of illnesses.

6. The word *pnigalion* ("throttling") used by the physician Themison and probably derived from the vernacular is based on a similar concept. The nightmare demon was most appropriately designated "the choker" or "strangler" and, in view of our previous exposition, this does not require any further explanation.

7. We have already dealt with all that is necessary for the understanding of *Epopheles* and *Opheles* ("helper," "savior"), testified by Soranus and Hesychius.

8. In the old commentaries on Aristophanes (*Wasps*, 1038) it says about the *epialoi kai puretoi* ("agues and fevers") whom Aristophanes

attacked as a second Heracles: "Didymus however says, 'The demon Epialos who is also called Epiales and *tiphus.'"* In place of the hitherto unexplained and difficult to understand *Euopan,* Rohde wishes to read *Euapana* (with reference to the *Suda*), which would of course excellently designate Pan, bleating like a he-goat, who frequently appears as a nightmare demon. Among the vase collections in the National Museum of Naples, there is one showing an actor or chorus member who is preparing himself for a satyr drama. He is crowned with ivy and wears around his loins the shaggy apron of the satyrs (*tragoi*) with tail and phallus. A clear parallel to this is the goat-footed Panisscos on the Etruscan bronze mirror from Preneste. Similarly the he-goat *koutsodaimonas* of the modern Greeks who attacks young girls and who, because of his horns, is dangerous to pregnant and post-parturient women, has the voice of a he-goat. Schmidt sees in him a direct descendant of the old Greek Pan. The following are to be quoted from the medieval and neo-Greek designations of the nightmare demon:

9. *Baruchnas,* noted by Eustathius and Psellus, together with the markedly deviating auxiliary forms *Barupnas, Braphnas, garupnas,* and *Brachnas* and *sbrachnas.* Sakellarios considers it a derivation from *barus* ("heavy") and *pneo* ("sleep") and understands barupnas to signify barupnous ("breathing hard"). Politis would prefer to consider it as a combination of *barus* and *hugnos.* The apparently irrational vowel changes are best explained by the noticeable tendency of superstitious people to alter arbitrarily the names of frightening demons because they fear the latter may cause mischief if called by their correct names. I can only say for certain that the adjective *barus* ("heavy"), which, as we have already seen, correctly designates an essential characteristic of the nightmare, is to be sought in this expression.

10. It is extremely difficult to establish the etymology of *baboutzias* and *baboutzikarios,* which first appear in later Byzantine literature. The first of these is found in a lexicon as an explanation of Ephialtes, according to du Cange (Charles du Fresne); the second is testified by the Suda and Mikhael Psellus in the work of Leo Allatius (*ephialtes: ho epi pollou baboutzias*). Since the distinguished family of the Baboutcicoi is mentioned by Joseph Genesius in the first half of the ninth century, both these designations of the nightmare must have arisen in the eighth century at the latest. Psellos thinks that the *baboutzikarios* is an evil spirit

that wanders around at Christmas time. Leo Allatius had already related this characteristic to the vampires of the later Greeks: that is a demon who sometimes appears as a werewolf, sometimes as a nightmare demon with the feet of a donkey or goat, with goat's ears and a hairy skin, and in many ways recalls the old Greek Pan and the satyrs who of course also appear as nightmare demons. Psellus has tried to connect the *baboutzi-karios* with Baubo, the mother of Damophon, known from the Demeter cult of Eleusis; this suggestion is however highly questionable. Perhaps the name is related to the modern Greek *papoutzas* ("shoemaker"), *papoutzion* ("slipper"), which, according to Littri, originated from the Arabic-Persian *baboudj, papoch* ("slipper"), and has been taken over by most modern languages (compare the French *babouche,* the German *Babusche* or *Papu(t)sche*). It is difficult to explain how the ideas of slipper or shoemaker are connected with the concept of a nightmare demon. It may however be pointed out that according to Grimm, a German hobgoblin who is also a nightmare demon is called "puss-in-boots" or simply "boot;" also as Sartori points out, there is occasionally talk of the slippers of the nightmare demons or night spirits, just as the dwarfs sometimes appear as shoemakers. Perhaps the demon itself is of Oriental origin, like his name. This is not surprising when one recollects the numerous and close connections between old Constantinople and the Orient.

11. Of the modern Greek words for the nightmare, *mora* is by far the most widely used. It seems to have taken its origin from the Slavic because the nightmare is called *mora* in Polish and *mura* in Bohemian. Grimm has connected it with the German *mar* (Anglo-Saxon *moere,* English "nightmare," French *cauchemar(e)*—from "trample upon," "squeeze"— and *mar* meaning nightmare). *Mora* is an epithet of the Gillou, a demon who chokes children, probably identical with the ancient Gello. The confusion between the demon of an illness causing children to choke (*paidopniktria*—"the one who strangles children") and the nightmare is not extraordinary when one remembers the *pavores nocturni,* which are, on the one hand, a pathological state and, on the other, are similar to nightmares.

This would seem an appropriate point to append the other titles for the nightmare found in classical writers, primarily in Latin.

12. The name *Inuus* stands out clearly as the oldest of all the Latin appellations of the nightmare. It first occurs in Virgil (*Aeneid,* 6.775), but

seems to be used here in the sense of the camp of Inuus. Its antiquity is also emphasized by Rutilius Namatianus. The ancients identified Inuus with Faunus (Pan) and liked to derive the name from *inire* in the sense of concumbere ("to lie together"). This seems hardly plausible on phonetic grounds because in this instance we should expect an earlier form *in-i-vus*. It seems much more probable that *Inuus* is no more than a word form that has arisen from the preposition "in" ("on," "upon," "to," "toward") by means of appending the suffix *-vus*, which after *n* had to change to *-uus* (compare *in-gen-uus*). One has to take for granted that this word form was employed for the nightmare demons in the very apt sense of "someone squatting or sitting on another," obviously in an erotic sense.

13. Closely related to *Inuus* in concept are the two terms In-cub-o and In-cub-us, which apparently classify the demon as the "sitter-on," i.e., a demonic being lying on the sleeper and being a burden. It should be noted at this point that *cubare, cubitare, concumbere, concubinus, concubitus*, etc., were used primarily for sexual intercourse and that therefore *incubo* and *incubus* sometimes have a decidedly erotic secondary meaning. The use of *incubus* and *succubus* in the sense of "paramour devil" is known in the Middle Ages. Generally speaking *incubus/-o* and *inuus* stand for an epithet of Faunus (Pan) or of Silvanus identified with Pan (faunus); on the other hand, incubus is also found as an appellative of Hercules in his role as the guardian of treasures and even appears once to have been thought of as a demon completely different from Faunus (Pan, Silvanus), who reveals or betrays treasures to the sleeper—just like the Greek Ephialtes—if the sleeper is able to rob him of his head covering. When incubo is used in the meaning of a guardian of treasures, it is well to note that *incubare* is often used of zealous watching, guarding money, or treasures, etc.

14. Since the first century CE, the term *fauni (fatui) ficarii* is repeatedly found for nightmare demons, as for example Cornelius Celsius in Pelagonius: "The horses are frequently disturbed at night by *faunus ficarius*; they are then afflicted by the most horrible pains and the restlessness often causes emaciation." Hieronymus in Esai writes: "Certain people call those whom many call fauni ficarii either incubi or satyres or silvestres (wood spirits)." According to Jordanis (who drew on Cassidor), the race of Huns originated from an intermixture of such *fauni ficarii* with witch-like women; and in old glossaries the Indo-Germanic word

vudevasan is explained with satyrs and *fauni ficarii*. (Grimm says that the nightmare demons, fairies, and witches appear as butterflies and especially as moths whose caterpillars naturally live on or near trees.) Du Cange correctly relates the adjective *ficarius* to fig trees in his glossary, while Bochart thinks of *ficus* in the sense of fig warts (the Greek *suke*), i.e., the small swellings on the necks of goats and satyrs (*pherea*, *verrucu/ae*), which commonly appear in imagery. Du Cange's view seems to be supported by Sicilian folk songs and Greek superstition, where even today fig trees are reputed to be the seats of evil spirits. Perhaps the indecent meaning of fig (*sukon*, Italian *fica*, French *figue*) is in context here. Compare also the Greek *sukazein* ("to gather ripe figs").

15. The designation *pilosus* belongs to about the same era as the name *faunus ficarius*. We first meet it in the Latin translation (*Vulgate*) of Isaiah (13: 20–21), where it says: "*Nec ponet ibi tentoria Arabs nec pastores requiescent ibi, sed requiescent ibi bestiae et replebuntur domus eorum draconibus, et habitabunt ibi struthiones, et Pilosi saltabunt ibi.*" (Authorized Version: "Neither shall the Arabian pitch tent there; neither shall the shepherds make their fold there. But wild beasts of the desert shall lie there, and dragons in their pleasant palaces, and owls shall dwell there, and satyrs shall dance there.") The Septuagint translates here: *kai daimonia ekei/orchesontai* ("and the demons shall dance there"), while the Hebrew original uses the word *seirim* (literally "goats") from which we are to understand goat-shaped demons, obviously akin to Pan, satyrs, and fauns, who live in lonely wildernesses and call to one another. That in fact nightmare demons are to be understood in the term *pilosi* follows not just from: "Fauni, however, are those whom the people call incubi or pilosi and who give answers when consulted by the pagans," but also from Isidore of Seville (*The Etymologies*, 8.11.103): "Pilosi ('the hairy ones") whom the Greeks call panitae, the Latins *incubi* or *inui* from indiscriminately copulating with animals, often indeed spring forth shamelessly; also to the women, and have intercourse with them. These demons the Gauls call by the name *dusii*, since they incessantly perform such filthiness." In addition, the old Bohemian glosses of Wacerad says: "The moruzzi *pilosi*, whom the Greeks call *panitae*, the Latins *incubi*, whose form is derived from the human but ends in the extremities of beasts." We may recollect here that in Polish and modern Greek, *mora* signifies the nightmare demon. As regards the *pilosi*, the fact that the fauns or

pilosi answer questions put to them shows that they are genuine night-mare demons. Obviously, the term *pilosi* specifies the nightmare demon as a rough-haired, shaggy being. This representation, as we have already seen, is quite simply explained by the rough-haired bedclothes made out of sheep and goat hides or wool. If these bedclothes impede the respiratory orifices of the sleeper, they will necessarily give rise to the concept of a rough-haired, goatlike nightmare demon. Thus we understand at the same time why the goat-shaped Pans, satyrs, and fauns necessarily came to be considered as nightmare demons: because in those days goatskins or sheep skins or cloaks made of goats' hair and sheep's wool were used to protect the sleepers from cold and inclement weather.

16. Finally, there remain the Gallic *dusii*. These were first mentioned by Augustinus and were characterized as nightmare demons lying in wait for women. Since almost all the evidence for these has already been carefully assembled by Alfred Holder (*Altceltischer Sprachschatz*, I: 1387ff.), I can justifiably dispense with reproducing it here. The dusii were thought to live in woods and on hills like the Pans, fauns, and sylphs. *Dusius* has now become "deuce." The word *dus-ii* is probably connected with the Greek *dus-*, Sanskrit *dus-*, Parsee *dush-i-ti* ("misery"), old Irish *du-*, and denotes the nightmare demons as wicked spirits. This explanation is in excellent agreement with the epithet *improbi* conferred upon them by Augustine and Isidore. Completely different, and to my mind, less applicable, is the etymology given by Holder who would like to connect it with the Lithuanian *dvaese* ("spirit," "soul"), the Slavonic *duchŭ,* and the Greek *theós*.

4

The Most Important of the Greek and Roman Nightmare Demons

As is already clear from our small collection of ancient nightmares, their creation was attributed to various gods and demons according to their widely varying content. Thus we see in no. 1 of our collection a goat-shaped being; in no. 2, a satyr; in nos. 3 and 5, spirits of the dead (heroes); in no. 4, human beings possessing demonic witchcraft; in no. 6, a siren; in no. 7, even Elohim; and in no. 8, Pan. In general it seems therefore, to judge from the few ancient nightmares depicted in more detail, that much the same holds true for them as for ordinary dreams: each god or demon—and in fact each demonic human being—is capable of causing nightmares and of appearing in them in his own shape or in another form. But although the number of divine or demonic originators of nightmares—and ordinary dreams—is almost unlimited, it is soon apparent on more exact investigation that there are really only a very few demons to whom the excitation of nightmares was ascribed. These demons have characteristics all their own. The fact that almost all gods and demons are possible producers of nightmares has probably misled Ludwig Laistner to see nightmare demons in all gods and demons and accordingly to elevate the nightmare to the chief and basic principle of all mythology.

We shall now consider each of these instigators and seek to answer the question: on what grounds has each individual one been regarded as a nightmare demon? Or, in other words, how can their relation to nightmares be explained from their other attributes and functions? (I have not considered here those nightmare demons who seem to be no more than personifications of the concept "nightmare" and of whom we really know only the names, e.g., Ephialtes, Tiphys, Incubo, Inuus, etc., because these have been dealt with in the preceding chapter. They play rather the same unimportant role as the dream demons in Ovid, e.g., Morpheus,

Phobetor or Icelus, Phantasus.) We shall begin our investigation with Pan who is the best known and most important of these demons. I conceive this god as the divine or demonic prototype of the old Greek shepherd and goat herdsman and as the incarnation of the collective ancient shepherds' life with all their experiences, customs, joys and sorrows.

1. *Pan.* Direct evidence for the significance of Pan as Ephialtes or exciter of nightmares first appears in the era of Augustus; nevertheless, on fundamental consideration of all relevant facts there can hardly be any doubt that the concept of Pan as a nightmare demon originated very much earlier, even in his original Arcadian home. (I have tried to show that the cult of Pan stems from Arcadia in *Archiv für Religionswissenschaften,* ed. T. Achelis [Leipzig und Tübingen, 1898], I: 54ff.) The evidence is as follows:

a. In the scholium on Aristophanes's *Wasps,* 1038: "Didymus says, 'a demon whom they call Ipialis or Typhis or Euapan.'"

b. Artemidorus (*Oneirocritica,* 2.37): "Ephialus, who has also been taken for Pan frequently, yet shows some differences: oppressive and heavy, he is the same in nightmares and terrors. However, whatever he answers is true. He grants various favors to those with whom he consorts, and he prophesies, particularly when he does not act as a nightmare. When he wishes them well, he cures the sick, but he never approaches the dying."

c. The interesting epigram of Hyginus in which it is avowed that he was cured of a severe illness by a vision of Pan-Ephialtes originates from the second century CE.

d. Augustine (*City of God,* 15.23): "The story is often repeated by people who have experienced it and by some who have heard it from eyewitnesses whose truthfulness is above doubt, that the Silvans and Pans, whom the people also call incubos, always carry on shamelessly with women, desire them and perform intercourse with them." We find virtually the same in Isidore of Seville (*Etymologies,* 8.11.103) and Gervase of Tilbury (*Otia Imperialia,* 3.86), both of whom are indebted to Augustine. The humorous legend by Ovid, incidentally, which is probably retold from the Alexandrine poets, is obviously based on this aspect of Pan. It begins with the words: "Twas midnight. What durst not wanton love essay?" Compare also pseudo-Heraclitus (*De incredibilibus,* 25): "On Pans and satyrs: They are born in the mountains and not used to women. If they meet a woman, they have intercourse with her. In great numbers they are wont to frighten the women into panicky terror."

The following considerations make it evident that these concepts of Pan-Ephialtes did not originate in the first century bce, but are much older. First of all Pan was at all times considered to be the initiator of all kinds of dreams and visions and especially the instigator of violent and sudden terror. Thus we know, for example, from Pausanias (2.32.6) about a sanctuary of *Pan Lytirius* ("Pan the redeemer") at Troezen, which was founded in memory of the town's liberation from an epidemic. Pan had revealed efficacious remedies to the town officials in their dreams. (The attested significance of Pan as a mantle god and teacher of Apollo in the art of divination in, e.g., the Lycosura and the arcadian Lyceum, can just as easily be traced back to a dream oracle as to Pan's function as the sender of mania, ecstasy, and *furor divinus*.) This clearly recalls the cure of Hyginus through a dream or vision of the god. The famous adventure of the herald Pheidippides, who immediately before the battle of Marathon claimed to have had a vision of the god on the Parthenian mountains at Tegea while he was on the way from Athens to Sparta, should presumably also be interpreted as a dream or vision. It then became the occasion for the establishment of the cult of Pan on the Acropolis at Athens. Furthermore, the *phasma* ("apparition"), which robbed Epizelus (or Polyzelus) of his eyesight in the battle of Marathon where Pan bestowed victory upon the Athenians by sending panicky terror.[85] was none other than an appearance of Pan according to the unknown informant of the *Suda*. (Whoever sees a god or the secret of a god against the god's will becomes blind or insane or dies. Compare the legends of Tiresias, Astrabacus, Aglaurus, Acteon, Semele.) Equally Longus[86] explains various dreadful visions and sound by day or night that cause panic as "revelations of Pan's anger with the sailors." This is expressly confirmed later by an appearance of the god in a dream that the leader of the fleet had during his midday sleep. How widespread was the concept that Pan when angry sends terrifying dreams and visions clearly appears from several glossaries of Hesychius and Photius, which have not been rightly understood until now. Photius (*Lexicon,* ed. Naber, 51): "Because Pan is the instigator of visions causing insanity;" Hesychus: "The emanations of Pan cause nightly visions." The anger of Pan is also frequently mentioned elsewhere, e.g., in the *Medea* by Euripides (1172), in relation to the onset of epilepsy. It can easily be recognized that the connection of Pan with dreams and visions—especially nightmares—is most intimately associated with panic, terror, the excitation of which was likewise ascribed to Pan.

I may be permitted here once again to state what I have already observed for the understanding of this remarkable phenomenon, which is easily comprehensible from the nature of Pan as the god of shepherds and herds: it is an acknowledged fact that even completely tame animals, such as sheep and goats, are affected by the most violent disquiet and terror, which frequently come on very suddenly—primarily during the night—and generally without any objectively perceptible reason. The animals become completely senseless, and as if insane, rush to one spot, even if this is highly dangerous for them. For example, they may charge into a precipice or into deep water and thus some animals or even the whole herd can perish. In Valerius Flaccus (*Argonautica,* 3.43ff.), the panicky terror that was fatal for the Doliones is traced to nocturnal trumpet calls and shouts of terror. The description runs: "Men's rest was broken; the god Pan had driven the doubting city distraught. Pan, lord of the woodlands and of war, whom caverns shelter from the daylight hours. About midnight in lonely places are seen that hairy flank and the roughing leafage in his fierce brow." The description ends with the words, "Sport it is to the god when he ravishes the trembling flock from their pens, and the steers trample the thickets in their flight."[87] The *Suda* says: "The terrors of Pan—something that occurs in military encampments; horses and men are suddenly thrown into agitation for no apparent reason; so called because these groundless terrors are attributed to Pan." Julius Fröbel writes on this panic of horses, dogs, etc.: "One of the most dangerous incidents that could happen on a journey is a night stampede, or to express myself in the classical manner, the effect of a panicky terror on a team of mules...The least misfortune to be feared is that one of the mule drivers will be trampled under foot by the team suddenly running away as if it were enraged. All the mules may be lost and the entire caravan perish" (*Beilage zur Allgemeinen Zeitung* [1890], no. 190). Modern zoologists have observed that goats and sheep in particular are subject to this terror, and one may remember also the panic that seized the herd of swine in the New Testament. Edward Burnett Tylor writes: "Animals shy and are startled where we cannot see any cause; do they perhaps see spirits which are invisible to me?"[88] This belief, which Tylor supports by several examples, demonstrates that not only acoustic but also, and just as frequently, visual phenomena bring on panicky terror in accordance with the ancient views.

The reader is invited to compare Dionysius (*Roman Antiquities,* 5.16): "For the Romans attribute panics to this divinity; and whatever apparitions come to men's sight, now in one shape and now in another, inspiring terror, or whatever supernatural voices come to their ears to disturb them, are the work, they say, of this god." These supernatural voices are the "ghost sounds of nature" about which E. Thiessen has recently published a stimulating article.[89] This is the so-called panicky terror of which the essential characteristic—as affirmed by the ancients—is the sudden unpredictable onset and the dangerous recklessness, heedless of all sense of reason, which attacks a number of individuals at the same time. Hence this is frequently called madness (*mania, pavor lymphaticus*). The Greek shepherds, naturally trying to explain the undoubtedly demonic character of this phenomenon (which, as has been said, frequently affected shepherd life) and to make it to some extent comprehensible, ascribed it to the destructive demonic action of Pan as the god of herds and shepherds. They were on their guard against arousing the anger of the god so that he might spare their herds from madness.

Thus Pan also becomes a god of war because he often sends panicky terror to large groups of people, particularly armies. This played a decisive part in ancient military history, as for example at Marathon and Delphi. The fact that the idea of panicky terror owes its origin primarily to the experiences and observations of shepherd life can also be seen in Aeneas Tacticus (*Poliorcetica,* 27), who states explicitly that *paneia* ("panic") has to be considered a Peloponnesian or Arcadian name, because Arcadia and the Peloponnese were held to be the true seat and original home of the cult of Pan from time immemorial.

For a deeper understanding of the close association between the two concepts of nightmare and panicky terror, I draw attention to 1) the epidemic nightmares already mentioned, which in their effects are fully on a par with panicky terror, and 2) the fact that elsewhere the demons inciting panicky terror are also identical with those of the nightmare. Thus, for example, a description of a stampede (i.e., the effect of panicky terror on the herds in the southwest of North America) says: "The herdsmen call this 'the nightmare' and attribute it to invisible powers, hobgoblins, or dwarfs who stupefy the cattle in this manner, frighten them, and drive them apart."[90] It was evidently taken for granted that animals as well as men were tormented in certain morbid states by terrifying dreams (nightmares) and hallucinations, which produced panicky terror. The most unequivocal evidence is found in the *Suda*: "Excitation through dreams: agitated by dreams, animals also fall ill, says Pythagoras;" and in Lucretius who says about the dreams of animals: "In truth you will see strong horses, when their limbs lie at rest, yet sweat in their sleep and go on panting and strain every nerve as though for victory."[91] The pathological condition mentioned here is undoubtedly identical with the one known to German superstition and outright ascribed to nightmare demons. Let us compare, for example, Wuttke:[92]

> Even horses and other animals are tormented by nightmares; the animals sweat profusely and snort loudly and become completely disarranged and have knotted manes, which cannot be combed out and can only be burned out with blessed candles or excised by a cut in the shape of a cross. The *Walriderske* (Westphalian and Oldenburg name for nightmare demons) ride on them to their business.

I presume that this very widespread illness of horses was actually called "nightmares," but for the present I cannot produce any definite proof for this designation. Snorting (*dyspnea*), sweating, and great unrest at night are also characteristic for nightmares afflicting humans, according to Soranus. It was indeed generally believed that horses and sheep suffered from almost the same illnesses as man. On this point see Aristotle: "Experience shows that almost all diseases affecting men also afflict horses and cattle."[93] The peculiar belief of the Huzuls that Kaindl tells us about certainly also belongs here:[94]

> At Christmas time these small devils (*szczezlyki, chowanci*) visit the stables and allow the cattle no peace. They ride and jump around on them so that the cattle die from exhaustion even during the night or become very emaciated; moreover, these devils break all the stable equipment to pieces. In order to prevent this, the stables must be fumigated with incense (*ladan*) in the evening and the locks of the doors bound with garlic, which keeps away all evil.

Very reminiscent of this is the story of the *Leetons*—the nightmare demons of the Latvians—where the horses are said to be ridden by the Maar or Leeton, as they are called, at night so that the horses become very feeble and tired; and they point out marks on some horses which are believed to have come from such riders. They put the head of a dead horse under the forage in the manger, because...this will chase off the Maars.

The Romans ascribed a similar illness to a wicked nightmare demon whom they called *Faunus ficarius*. The signs of this illness were emaciation, violent unrest at night, and agonizing pains. The Greeks knew the same type of demon who made horses timid and restless and called him Taraxippus. This demon was venerated in the hippodromes in Olympia, on the Isthmus, and at Nemea. As a rule he was considered a hero, i.e., an ill-natured spirit of the dead, but other interpretations took him to be, for example, the giant Ischenus, other giants and titans, and even Poseidon. The question about the nature of Taraxippus entered a new stage through the interesting essay by Pernice on an old Corinthian picture that shows a dwarflike, beardless, and definitely erotic demon who stands behind the rider at the base of the horse's tail and clasps his very prominent phallus with both hands. (An "apelike squatting" teasing spook is said to be found on a vase from Tragliatella, but this was not accessible to me.) He is almost certainly a Taraxippus. We see a demon of similar build on another ancient Corinthian slab in which he stands in front of a potter's oven. Considering the erotic character of this demon, various completions are possible; most of them would translate as libidinous, wanton; rake and perversion are also possible. Pernice has interpreted this as one of the malicious *Kobolds* who, according to the Homeric pottery blessing (*kaminos he kerameis*), create mischief in the potter's oven by wrecking the vessels. Robert[95] already considered these oven *Kobolds* to be a type of satyr. This could be correct, although all the characteristics borrowed from the goat or horse are absent in the demon portrayed on the Corinthian slab. As Furtwängler first recognized, grotesque dancers with conspicuously enormous bellies and pelvis and often a huge penis appear in ancient Corinthian ceramics in place of the here completely unknown satyrs and silenes, who are very like the Taraxippus and this oven *Kobold*. We may, moreover, take this opportunity to recollect that in Sophocles's satyr play *Heracles at Taenarum* helots take the place of the satyr. In the Corinthian satyrlike potbellies one automatically thinks of Hesiod's[96] coarse characterization of the uneducated, uncouth shepherd: "Shepherds sleeping in the open, consisting of stomachs only, dastardly scoundrels." When one considers that the nightmare demons of the Huzuls also disturb horses and wreck the equipment of the stables, the idea suggests itself that the two phallic dwarflike *Kobolds* on the Corinthian picture are basically those mischievous nightmare demons who at times make horses shy or become ill and sometimes operate in the potter's oven to the detriment of its owner. Compare also the similar appearances of malicious dwarfs and *Kobolds* described in Grimm's *German Mythology*. The strongly marked phallic character of these spirits speaks for this interpretation; the characteristic explains itself easily by the unmistakable erotic trait proper to all night mare demons. In addition, there is the observation of the ancients that dwarfs have large genitals. Aristotle says:[97] "The mule, like the dwarfs, also has a large private part." The presentation of such dwarfs (pygmies) in art correspond to this idea. It is true that the common identity of Taraxippus and Pan cannot be proven. The former seems to have more in common with the satyrs than with Pan because he is still lacking the goat horns and feet, which are specific to Pan. Nevertheless we may take it for granted that there was an inner relationship between these two demons based on the common connection to the erotic nightmare and to panicky terrors, i.e., the shying of animals.

On the other hand, the reports of the remarkable modern Greek demon called *laboma,* which means "harm" or "bane" and lives on even today in the beliefs of the shepherds of Parnassus, have to be considered as undoubted reminiscences of the ancient representations of the nature and actions of Pan. Bernhard Schmidt says:[98] "This being is in the habit of mounting goats in the form of a he-goat and bringing about their sudden death. Many shepherds from the Parnassus claim to have been eyewitnesses of this and say that the animals are seized by excruciating pains during copulation with the demon, shriek fearfully, and die after a short time. Sometimes the demon simulates the usual call or the pipes of the herdsman leading the herds and thus lures the unsuspecting animals to himself. Nobody dares to fire his gun or pistol when he is aware of the demon because many a weapon has exploded and caused a fatal wound to the shooter." Schmidt asserted with great emphasis the fact that because the Corycian Cave was already dedicated to Pan and to the nymphs in ancient times, and was always a secure place of refuge for the shepherds of Parnassus and their flocks, and because Pan was considered and even portrayed as an attacker like the present-day demon, we must therefore perceive in the goat-demon of contemporary Parnassian shepherds just one particular metamorphosis of Pan. The validity of this assumption seems beyond doubt, particularly as we have just seen that demons ascribed to the nightmare are frequently held responsible for certain fatal illnesses in cattle, manifesting themselves in multifarious ways in frightful excitement and unrest; we can assume that these demons in such cases rode or jumped on these animals. With the familiar secondary erotic meaning of these words, they obviously stand for copulation (compare the Latin *salire, inire,* the Greek *thornistai,* etc.). As regards the riding habits of the nightmare demons, I refer to Grimm.[99]

In closest association with these views of Pan as a nightmare demon and exciter of panicky terrors as well as certain veterinary diseases is the fact that he was also considered to be the originator of epilepsy and mental illness. Definitive evidence for the ancient beliefs on Pan's relation to epilepsy is found in the *Medea* of Euripides where it says of the onset of Creusa's disease (caused by the poisoned garment of Medea) that to begin with the illness gave the impression of an epileptic attack brought about by Pan, in so far as the sudden rigors, the falling on the ground, and the pallor are the three main signs of epilepsy. The ancient scholiast already summed up the position when he remarked of the words "That frenzy was of Pan or some god sent" that "men assumed from time immemorial that those who suddenly fell (the epileptics) were deranged by Pan or Hecate." Recognizing the inner connection between such epileptic attacks and panicky terror and the sudden mental disturbances arising from it, he adds further: "The reason for sudden frights and mental disturbances they ascribe to Pan." Modern medicine also holds that a sudden violent terror frequently produces spasmodic forms of epilepsy, St. Vitus's dance, asthma, and indeed even mental disturbance. Abortion following a sudden shock also belongs in this context. This gave rise to the theory that the demons of panicky terror are dangerous to pregnant and puerperal women and that they cause the feared puerperal fever with its attendant delirium. Aretaeus of Cappadocia has observed with remarkable accuracy that many epileptics imagine directly before the attack that they are being persecuted by a horrible wild animal or a ghost and have all kinds of evil and strange dreams as well as peculiar aural hallucinations that remind us of the visual and acoustic phenomena of Pan's anger in Longus. It is interesting that Hippocrates does not mention Pan among the demons to whom popular belief ascribed the origin of epilepsy (Cybele, Poseidon, Enoida [= Hecate], Apollon Nomios [?], Ares, the Heroes). The reason is probably that in the time of Hippocrates the cult of the ancient Arcadian shepherd god had not yet extended to the island of Cos and the coast of Asia Minor.

Pan, as author of severe and sometimes fatal epileptic attacks, which occasionally were not convulsive and could then give the impression of death, could eventually become a vicious death demon, as is shown by an incantatory tablet found in a grave near Constantine. These tablets were inscribed with a curse and buried in a grave to establish contact with the Underworld. The inscription says: "He (the one to be cursed) shall be carried away, so that you (the death demon) shall make him devoid of feeling, memory, breath, that he shall become a shadow of himself."[100] The rest is illegible. The demon portrayed on the tablet is described by Wunsch as follows: "In the ancient times the demon who was invoked had the split hairy hoofs of a he-goat and was armed with two slings and a hook."[101] Loss of feeling, consciousness, memory, speech, and withholding of the breath are familiar symptoms of epilepsy, and it is therefore my conjecture that it is not improbable to consider Pan, in the form of the goat-footed demon, as the originator of nightmares and epileptic fits. In conclusion we may once again recollect the view of Soranus that the nightmare is incipient epilepsy. This claim, as we have just seen, now appears to be quite natural and also comprehensible from the viewpoint of ancient popular belief.

Thus Pan finally developed into being an originator of mental disturbance (*mania*). (Incidentally, I would like to draw attention to how closely related the two concepts of mania and epilepsy are.) As such Pan appears in the writings of Euripides, who in *Hippolytus* makes the chorus say to the love-frenzied Phaedra:

> Maiden, thou must be possessed, by Pan made frantic or by Hecate,
> or by the Corybantes dread, and Cybele the mountain mother.

The scholiast adds: "Enthusiasts are those whose reason has been robbed by an apparition and who are possessed by the god who has appeared to them and executed his orders." This observation of the ancient commentator is psychologically quite correct in so far as hallucinations, visions, and illusions are in fact the surest sign of mental illness and first appear in the dreams of the insane; this fact is in complete harmony with the observation made in ancient times that heavy dreams—and nightmares in particular—precede the onset of epilepsy and insanity. Thus it can be easily understood how Pan, the agent of nightmares, visions, hallucinations, and epileptic attacks had to become the originator of mental diseases. Two further facts contributed to this: the first is the experience of a sudden violent fright, as the *phasmata* of Pan usually cause, frequently producing not merely epileptic fits but severe mental disturbances as well; the second is the panicky terror of animals and men, interpreted as mania or fits of rage and therefore attributed to the demons who elsewhere, too, induced madness or insanity according to the ancient point of view. This fact is further elucidated by the passage in the synoptic gospels[102] where Jesus cast out a legion of devils who had possessed a man, and their unclean spirits entered into a herd of two thousand swine. The swine were then possessed by such panicky terror that "the herd ran violently down a steep place into the sea and were choked in the sea." On the other hand there is the story of Pausanias (10.23.7) about the panicky terror that befell the Gauls under Brennus at Delphi in the year 278 BCE, which was actually called *mania*.

In order to justify further the equal position of panicky terror and insanity in the classical period, I should like to draw attention to the relative frequency of epidemic nightmares and insanity, i.e., that a large number of individuals succumb at the same time, which again resembles panicky terror. In the following passage we learn of such an instance of epidemic insanity in the form of cynanthropy or pycanthropy traced back to Pan, where it says of Pan and Echo: "Pan is enraged with the girl because he envies her music and because he is ugly. He cements the shepherds and goat herdsmen. They tear the girl apart like wolves or dogs and throw her limbs in all directions. The limbs however go on singing."[103] There is also further evidence of Pan being the inciter of insanity elsewhere. If we refer to my article in the *Rheinisches Museum für Philologie* 53 (1898), 199, we shall find several other cases of this type of epidemic insanity and also proof that the illness of the daughters of Pandareus (*Odyssey,* 20.66ff.) mentioned by the scholiast was most probably cynanthropy (lycanthropy).

I shall conclude this consideration of Pan-Ephialtes with its expressed objective of specifying as completely as possible the reasons why the ancient Arcadian shepherd god became a nightmare demon—by alluding to the erotic impulse attributed to him at all times and especially in innumerable sculptures. One should remember his roughhaired, he-goat image, which he shares with other nightmare demons, because, as we have seen, the usual bedding in ancient times was the skin of a goat or cloth made of goat's hair, which by its very nature must have conjured up the appearance of goat-like nightmare demons in the person afflicted with the nightmare. We may think of the appearance of the he-goat to Sinonis, the satyr in Philostratus, appearing as a nightmare demon—probably also in semi-goat form—and finally we may remember the Germanic *Bocksmahrte* (lit. "he-goat nightmare"), the *Hafergeiss* (lit. "oat-goat," presumably from the erotic connotation of oats; cf. the English "to sow wild oats"), and lastly the he-goat as the mount of the Murawa and Trude.

2. *Satyrs.* As we have already seen, the satyrs sometimes appear as nightmare demons in absolutely genuine erotic nightmares. This is easily understandable because in this respect as in many other ways the satyrs are closely related to Pan whose image they represent, distorted into the vulgar, comical, burlesque, and mischievous. The satyrs also originated in Argos. Like Pan, they are goat-shaped demons; their relation to him is virtually the same as that of the little Pans who—as is evident from Wernicke's collection of illustrations on vases—are visually completely identical with the satyrs and are constantly mistaken for them in modern descriptions. The word he-goat is equally suitable for both of them. The position is similar with the so-called "horned satyrs" who frequently cannot be differentiated from the human-legged Pan. They have the partial or complete shape of a goat in common with Pan, as is evident from their permanent designation he-goat or *titiros* (actually a long-tailed monkey) and from their representation on ancient Attic vases with red figures, which have been excellently dealt with by Wernicke (*Hermes* XXXII, 297ff.). Furthermore, they are shaggy and possess an irresistible erotic impulse. These characteristics are all common to other nightmare demons, too. Compare also the satyr Lasios of the Munich drinking bowl, and the names of satyrs found on vases: Peos ("phallos"), Sybas ("sybarite"), Stygon ("erector"), Poston ("little tail"), Eraton ("lecher"). In other respects, however, they closely resemble the above mentioned *Kobolds* of the Germans and other northern races, who also

frequently appear as nightmare demons. Here belongs their pronounced propensity to all kinds of practical jokes and pranks which they would even play against the mighty Hercules. Moreover, there is their passion for stealing, plundering, and deceiving, just like the wicked *Kobolds* are wont to do. The *cercops* are very similar in their nature. They are also incapable of any work; they are plunderers and thieves. Their lasciviousness is probably expressed in their very name (*kerkos* = *phallus*). I shall not venture a guess about monkeys' tails because, as far as I know, these are missing on the sculptures, although the *cercops,* like the satyrs and Pan, are connected with monkeys. Lobeck has combined them with the *kobaloi,* a type of demon in the following of Dionysus, as belonging to the sphere of these burlesque and multifariously spiteful *Kobold*-like nightmare demons. However, at present there is no definitive evidence that they are connected with the nightmare.

3. *Faunus.* It cannot be my task here to prove that Faunus in his origin and basic meaning is very close to Pan. This is to say that, just like Pan, he is an ancient demon of shepherds (peasants) and herds and because of his obvious similarity to the old Arcadian shepherd was placed on a par with Pan at the first contact of Greek religion with the religion of the Romans. I must content myself here with showing that Faunus became a nightmare demon for exactly the same reasons as Pan. While appealing to the evidence for the validity of Faunus as a nightmare demon communicated above, I shall draw attention primarily to the fact that Faunus is wont to reveal himself exactly like Pan in prophetic dreams and in all kinds of optical and acoustic visions, especially of the fearful variety. How old and widespread was the belief in Faunus as a sender of prophetic dreams appears evident from the incubation rites described by Virgil[104] about an oracle of Faunus in a sacred grove that surrounded the source of the Tiburtine sybil Albunea. Likewise in Ovid[105] these rites had to be observed if a revelation in a dream was desired from Faunus: First of all, sheep had to be sacrificed and then the pilgrims had to lie down to sleep on the skins of the slaughtered animals in the grove sacred to Faunus. In addition, a coronation with beech leaves, chastity, abstinence, and the removal of finger rings were necessary. In most primitive races a frugal diet or fasting is the chief means for securing visions and prophetic dreams, as is evident from the excellent observations of Tylor. This ritual, as Preller[106] rightly notes, gives the impression of being very

ancient indeed and agrees strikingly with the Greek customs of incubation. I do not know how Marquardt[107] came to the conclusion that the Roman incubation rite came into use only late and originated in Greece. At all events, the most competent authority on this facet of very ancient religions, Bouché-Leclercq,[108] takes it for granted, with good justification, that the dream oracle of Pan Lyterios of Troizen is concerned with incubation. If this assumption is correct, the parallel existing between Pan and Faunus is increased by an important point.

Even more numerous are the testimonies for the belief that Faunus—just as Pan—displays himself in optical and acoustic phenomena of all kinds, which for the most part produce horror. The main passage on this point is found in Dionysius of Halicarnassus[109] and runs: "For the Romans attribute panics to this divinity; and whatever apparitions come to men's sight, now in one shape and now in another, inspiring terror, or whatever supernatural voices come to their ears to disturb them, are the work, they say, of this god." Notice how the acoustic and optical phenomena of Faunus are linked with panicky terror, which, after what I have just said about Pan, is easily comprehensible and affords a gratifying confirmation of the explanation I have given here. Possibly the words of Lucretius relate to the acoustic phenomena of Faunus: "People affirm that the peace of night is broken by the noisy rampaging and play of the fauns." However, it cannot be excluded that this concept is of Greek origin and borrowed from Pan and the satyrs, who are mentioned directly beforehand together with the nymphs. The characterization of Picus and Faunus given by Plutarch (*Numa,* 15) in connection with the familiar ancient Roman legend where Numa overpowers these two demons, says that, as genuine nightmare demons, "they renounce their own nature by taking up various forms and shapes and conjure up terrifying visions before men's eyes. They predict much of the future and inform men about it," particularly when they are sodden with wine and held fast. Similarly, Ovid[110] says of the dream god Icelos or Phobetor: "[He] takes the form of beast or bird or the long serpent. Him the gods call Icelus, but mortals name him Phobetor." Compare also Ludwig Laistner's *Riddle of the Sphinx,* 1: 62ff., 87ff., 92f., and 2: 4f., on the metamorphoses of nightmare demons. Other nightmare demons can also be induced to prophesy and impart useful instruction or perform useful services if they are intoxicated with wine or are seized and held fast. That these concepts of Faunus are not borrowed from the cult and myth of the Greek Pan, but are of genuine Italian origin is primarily guaranteed by the very old historic legend of the battle in the wood Arsia where either Faunus or Silvanus—like to him in nature and therefore identified with him—inspired the enemy with panicky terror by nightly acoustic phenomena and thus decided the issue in favor of the Romans. The belief of the Roman people in the acoustic and visual phenomena of Faunus was indeed so deep-rooted that one could even venture to explain the name of the god on this basis: According to Servius,[111] Faunus was to be derived from the Greek phone = "utterance," while Hesychius interprets the name from *phainon anion* = "the one who shows himself." Other sources attribute the same significance to the visual as to the acoustic phenomena of Faunus. We have already seen that attempts were made to derive Pan from *phainein* = "show" on the same grounds.

Certain equine illnesses with emaciation and nocturnal unrest for symptoms were also attributed to Fatuus ficarius, i.e., Faunus, as a nightmare demon. These have already been discussed. The following prayer of Horace[112] directed to him shows that he was generally thought of as both sender of and protector against animal diseases, in particular those of young sheep and kids:

> Across my farm in sunshine bright
> Come gently, and retire from sight
> Kind to my cattle's young.

Porphyrion explains here: "He invokes Faunus who is said to be a low and pestilential god." Compare also Acron on this passage: "the young calves, which the Fauns are said to harm most" and Servius: "Horace represents Faunus as injurious, saying: "Come gently.""

There is no direct tradition that Faunus was like Pan held to be the producer of insanity, but this is not improbable when we consider that the mantle ecstasy or divination inspiration was at all times interpreted as "frenzy" (*furoris divinalis*),[113] just as prophecy through dreams was always connected with Faunus (*Faluus*) and his wife Fauna (Faina). Faunus therefore received the appellatives *fatidicus*,[114] *Fatuclus,* and *Faluus* ("prophet"); and the oldest sayings and prophesies of the inhabitants of Italy in the saturnal or "faunish" scansion were attributed to him. I have perceived in this a definite parallel to Pan, who dispensed oracles "from time immemorial" and whose prophetess is said to have been the nymph

Erato, the wife of Arcas. A collection of prophecies comparable to those of the sibyls circulated under her name even as late as Pausanias that Dionysius Periegetes claimed to have read himself.

Finally, the familiar relationship to he-goats characterized by hirsuteness and a strongly pronounced erotic impulse can be called upon to prove the development of the ancient Italian god of shepherds and their herd, Faunus, into a nightmare demon. We cannot prove definitely that Faunus, even before being equated with Pan, was represented as a mixture of goat and man (that is, with a goat's horns and legs) like Pan, but it is certain that his ancient Roman "wolf priests", the Luperci, were called "creppi," i.e., he-goats, because they were clothed only in goat skins, and that Faunus himself was represented pictorially in this attire, which reminds one of that of the satyrs who were equally called he-goats. The sacrifice of male and female goats which was customary in the cults of both Pan and of Faunus is of course closely associated.

4. *Silvanus.* The forest god Silvanus arose from an almost identical sphere of thought and experience as Faunus and Pan. The similarity with these gods was so obvious to the ancients that Silvanus was sometimes identified with one and sometimes with the other. According to Probius[115] writing on Virgil, the shepherd Crathis fathered the goat-shaped Silvanus with a goat. Aelianus[116] tells the same legend about the birth of Pan. The myth is of Sybarite origin; the Sybarites however came partly from Achaia (where there was also a river called the Crathis) and partly from Troizen and consequently from the original home of the cult of Pan. The equation of Silvanus and Faunus is also testified to by Aurelius.[117] It seems from the legend of the battle of the Arsian wood that this equation is very old. Sometimes it is Faunus and sometimes Silvanus who is credited as the demonic caller and originator of the panicky terror. The essential similarity to Pan and Faunus is further shown in the fact that, like them, Silvanus became a nightmare demon. This is evident in Augustine: "There is also a very general rumor, which many have verified by their own experience, or which trustworthy persons who have heard the experience of others corroborate, that sylvans and fauns, who are commonly called *incubi*, had often made wicked assaults upon women and satisfied their lust upon them."[118] Again, like Pan and Faunus, Silvanus was held to be an originator of panicky terror, particularly through acoustic phenomena; hence the terror-awakening call in the battle in

the Arsian wood was sometimes ascribed to Silvanus and sometimes to Faunus. Varro (as quoted by Augustine) suggests the belief that Silvanus also brought about the terrifying visions and dangerous deliria of puerperal fever when he says: "Post-parturient women are watched over by three gods so that Silvanus should not break in at night and vex them. In order to signify these guardians, three men patrol the threshold at night and first hit the threshold with an axe followed by a pestle and finally sweep the threshold with a broom. These signs show that the house is occupied and should prevent Silvanus from entering. For neither can trees be felled and cut without iron, nor can corn be prepared without a pestle, nor can the harvest be heaped up without the broom. From these three things the gods derive their names: Intercidona from the fall of the axe, Pilumnus from the pestle (*pilus*), and Deverra from the broom. The powers of these three gods guard the post-parturient woman from the god Silvanus." Augustine adds further: "Therefore the watch of the just would not prevail against the wrath of the malicious god if there were not several against one to repulse him, who is rough, uncultivated, and repugnant, as from the woods, with the signs of cultivation which are opposed to his nature."[119] (Possibly the "certain illnesses" of the moonstruck [somnambulists] in Macrobius[120] partly relate to puerperal fevers, in particular where fatal illnesses are concerned. The belief that post-parturient women were especially endangered by wicked demons and must be protected against them is very widespread indeed.) It was obviously taken for granted that the same demon who importuned women in nightmares also appeared to them in the deliria of puerperal fever and could become dangerous. The same is true of the goat-shaped *koutsodaimonas* of the modern Greeks, who most probably corresponds to the ancient Greek Pan. He has "a very long chin with a beard (goat's beard), his eyes are embedded in wiry hair, and he has the voice of a goat. He not only assaults young girls, but is also dangerous to post-parturient and pregnant women because he butts their abdomens with his horns"[121]

Not only the post-parturient women but also the newborn infants were believed to be in danger from Silvanus, as is evident from a fragment of Varro: "If the child is born alive and has been picked up by the midwife, it is laid on the ground to ensure favorable auspices; an offering is prepared in the house for Pilumnus and Picumnus, the gods of matrimony." Servius comments on Virgil, *Aeneid* 10, 76: "Varro attests that Pilumnus and Picumnus are the gods of newborn infants and that an offering is prepared for them in the atrium on behalf of the post-parturient woman to enquire whether the newborn baby is fit to sur-vive." We see here that Pilumnus and Picumnus had to protect not only the mother but her newborn infant as well. There would also seem to have been a belief that Silvanus abducted and exchanged children (changelings), which is supported by the superstition still current in the South Tyrolean Fassa Valley that the *Salvegn* (= Silvani) frequently exchange children.

As a final point it is worth noting that Silvanus also corresponds to Pan and Faunus in that he, too, sometimes takes on the form of a he-goat, receives goats as sacrifical victims, and is rough-haired and shaggy; all these characteristics have contributed to no small degree to his develop-ment into a nightmare demon.

The old Indian nightmare demons, the Gandharves and Rakshas, show a remarkable similarity to Pan, Faunus, Silvanus, and the satyrs. Covered in hides and skins, they dance and rage in the woods in the evening, they avoid the daylight; they skip around the houses, braying like a donkey. Taking on the shape of a brother or father, or muffled up, or in hideous deformity, they appear hunchbacked and humped, flabby bellied with excessive torso, black hair, bristly, unkempt, and with the stench of a goat. The most effective antidote against them is a yellow, strong-smelling herb—Baja or Pinga or Ayacringi (goatshorn)—which plays the same part as the peonies in Greek and Roman superstition. They lie in wait for sleeping women, at the wedding procession, at the first nuptials, and just after childbirth; they haunt the women as licen-tious, permanently excited sex spirits with large testicles, and they enjoy killing newborn infants. They abide in darkly shaded places (cf. Silvanus) and they are capable of driving women into a frenzy. They are rough-haired and hence compared with monkeys and dogs. Their female coun-terparts are the Apsaras, who are comparable to the elves, nymphs, and sirens and are almost the same as the Gandharves.

85. Herodotus, 6.117.

86. Longus, Pastorales, 2.25 and 26.

87. W. H. Roscher, *Selene und Verwandtes* (Leipzig: B.G. Teubner, 1890), 157ff.

88. E. B. Tylor, *Die Anfänge der Cultur: Untersuchungen über die Entwicklung der Mythologie, Philosophie, Religion, Kunst und Sitte* (Leipzig: C. F. Winter'sche Verlagshandlung, 1873), 197ff.

89. E. Thiessen, "Gespensterlaute in der Natur," *Die Woche* (Berlin, 1900), vol. 2, no. 20: 878ff.

90. "Eine Stampede auf den Weideflächen im südwestlichen Nordamerika," *Illustrierte Zeitung*, no. 2821 (Leipzig and Berlin, 22 July 1897): 122.

91. Translation by H. A. J. Munro, 1908, ed. 1947.

92. Wuttke, *Der deutsche Volksaberglaube der Gegenwart* (Berlin: Wiegandt & Grieben, 1900), par. 403.

93. Aristotle, *Historia Animalium*, 8.24.

94. R. F. Kaindl, "Zauberglaube bei den Huzulen," *Globus* 76 (1899): 255.

95. See "Die Satyrn," in L. Preller, *Griechische Mythologie*, vol. I (Berlin: Weidmansche Buchhandlung, 1894), 726ff.

96. Hesiod, *Theogonia*, 26.

97. Aristotle, *Historia Animalium*, 6.24.

98. B. Schmidt, *Das Volksleben der Neugriechen und das hellenische Alterthum* (Leipzig: B.G. Teubner, 1871), 1:156.

99. J. Grimm, *Deutsche Mythologie* (Göttingen: Dieterichsche Buchhandlung, 1835), 384ff.

100. *Corpus Inscriptionum Latinarum*, vol. VIII supp., pars II, n. 19525 (= Eph. V, n. 896)

101. *Defixionum tabellae Atticae / collegit, collectas praemissa praefatione*, ed. R. Wünsch, in Inscriptiones Graecae, vol. 3: Corpus inscriptionum Atticarum, pars 3 (Berlin: Reimer, 1897), xxvi.

102. Mark 5:1–14; Matthew 8:28ff.; Luke 8:26ff.

103. Longus, *Pastorales*, 3.23.

104. Virgil, *Aeneid*, 7.81ff.

105. Ovid, *Fasti*, 4.641.

106. L. Preller, *Römische Mythologie* (Berlin: Weidmannsche Buchhandlung, 1881), 1:383.

107. J. Marquardt, *Römische Staatsverwaltung* (Leipzig: Verlag von S. Hirzel, 1878), 3:97ff.

108. A. Bouché-Leclercq, *Histoire de la Divination dans l'Antiquité* (Paris: Ernest Leroux, 1880), 2:386.

109. Dionysius of Halicarnassus, *Roman Antiquities*, 6.16.

110. Ovid, *Metamorphoses*, 2.638ff.

111. Servius, on the *Aeneid*, 7.81.

112. Horace, *Carmina*, 3.18, 295 (trans. Lord Dunsany [London, 1947]).

113. Cicero, *De Divinatione*, 1.2.4.
114. Virgil, *Aeneid*, 7.82.
115. Probius, *Georgics*, 1.20.
116. Aelianus, *De Natura Animalium*, 6.42.
117. [Aurelius Victor], *De Viris Illustribus*, 4.
118. Augustine, *De Civitate Dei*, 15.23 (trans. M. Dods).
119. Ibid., 6.9.
120. Macrobius, *Saturnalia*, 1.17.2.
121. Schmidt, *Das Volksleben der Neugriechen*, 1:153ff.

Bibliographical Endnote

The title page of the original monograph is printed as follows:

EPHIALTES,

EINE PATHOLOGISCHE-MYTHOLOGISCHE ABHANDLUNG

ÜBER DIE

ALPTRÄUME UND ALPDÄMONEN

DES KLASSISCHEN ALTERTUMS

VON

WILHELM HEINRICH ROSCHER

Des XX. Bandes der Abhandlungen der philologisch-historischen Classe der
Königl. Sächsischen Gesellschaft der Wissenschaften

№ II

—

LEIPZIG

BEI B.G. TEUBNER

1900

The monograph consisted of 123 pages of text (plus a "systematic" table of contents, i.e., a digest of contents, and an index). Here, 92 pages have been translated together with most of the 285 footnotes that have been, for the most part, lifted into the text. The translations of the classical passages have been mainly—but not in every case—ours. The reader who wishes to pursue any reference in detail may consult either an English version of the Classical author or the original Greek and Latin. The references have been generally adapted to the standard English abbreviations, which preface *The Oxford English Dictionary,* the *Greek-English Lexicon* of Liddell and Scott, and the *Latin Dictionary* of Lewis and Short. The three short appendices that have not been included in this edition are: I. "The Meaning of the Name Mephistopheles," in which Roscher concludes that the Medieval and Renaissance Devil is not only figuratively but also etymologically connected with the nightmare-Pan demon; II. "Passages from Ancient Physicians on the Nature and Origin of Nightmares," which presents in the light of results obtained in the monograph, improved texts (in Latin and Greek) of everything concerning the nightmare in the works of ancient physicians (Soranus, Oribasius, Aetius, etc.); III. A Latin quotation from Trithemius (*Annales Hirsaugiensis* II) from the seventeenth century on nightmare demons who possessed cloistered nuns. Finally, pages 120–23 contain, in small print, Roscher's "Nachträge," or postscript comments, internecine scholarly arguments, corrections, and afterthoughts to the work as a whole. It was customary then to include additional information gathered subsequent to the printing of the first sheets in such a "Nachtrag," so that the work would be as up-to-the-minute and completely authoritative as possible.

—J.H.

Made in the USA
Columbia, SC
07 March 2021